WHAT IS THE NEW AGE?

WHAT IS THE NEW AGE?

Michael Cole, Tony Higton, Jim Graham, David C. Lewis

HODDER AND STOUGHTON
LONDON SYDNEY AUCKLAND TORONTO

British Library Cataloguing in Publication Data

What is the new age?
  1. Christianity
  I. Cole, Michael *1934–*
200

   ISBN 0-340-52912-1

Contents

Foreword

The recent upheavals in Eastern Europe and Russia have seen the discarding of Marxism – one of the crowning expressions of the age of materialism. Our world is entering an era of 'spirituality'. Many who commence the spiritual journey do so with little knowledge about its topography. There is an easy assumption that anything spiritual must be good. In fact nothing could be further from the truth. There is a spiritual kingdom of darkness which can masquerade as light. Discernment is called for. All that glistens is not gold. Even the elect may be deceived by appearances and adopt forbidden and unbiblical practices. This was the tragic side of Israel's history in the Old Testament. Western Christians need to be aware of different, yet similar, dangers today.

Many Christians are confused by the subtle recycling of the Eastern World View they are encountering today. 'New Age theories, therapies and activities are working their way into our economic, corporate, cultural, social, academic, political and religious life' (Russell Chandler). How are we to assess what we see around us? We want neither to wander into any New Age trap nor to throw out the baby of true spirituality in Christ with the New Age bath water. Yet, some Bible-loving Christians appear to be making sweeping condemnations. Anything supernatural is suspect and branded as New Age, and the teaching of some of today's leading Christians has been targeted – and all too often the results have been slanderous and the damage great.

Some months ago we called a conference for Church leaders at St Andrew's, Chorleywood, to consider current New Age teaching. David Wavre, the editor of Hodder and

Stoughton, heard the tapes and suggested a book. This joint effort is the outcome. It should help people on the British scene to discern some of the fundamental issues, which cannot be confined to denominational boundaries, and also to see why we reject the New Age. The book is written by mature Christian leaders, who bring their own special skills and insights to the subject. I believe you will find the book interesting, helpful, stimulating, vital and timely!

David Pytches

1

Defining the New Age

The Ubiquity of the New Age

You will come across the New Age almost anywhere: airport news-stands, station bookstalls, the local news-agents, and the 'freebie' that is dropped through the letter-box.

It is unusual and influential enough to excite plenty of media interest. For example, *Time* magazine (19th January 1987) described the New Age movement as 'an esoteric blend of computer-age jargon and ancient religious prac-tice, which often invested stones with powerful magic'. The *Sunday Times* (29th October 1989) contained an article by Kate Saunders in its 'Style and Society' section, headed 'All you need is self-love. Are New Age values here to stay as the eighties fade away?' Ms Saunders writes:

Age is rapidly becoming a fashionable buzzword among nitted style warriors. Last year's smart woman was a k piranha in a tight black suit, fond of bitching over a glass of champagne. Next year she will be a spiritual creature in a simple white robe, empathising over a pottery mug of herbal tea. Around her neck will hang a crystal, and not just for ornament. Crystals, it is claimed, can improve meditation, restore inner peace and even record information.

The *Mail on Sunday* (16th July 1990) carried an article entitled 'Soul and Heal'. It began: 'Ayurveda is a holistic approach to health care that has been around for 3,000 years. It is now being promoted in the West by the man who brought transcendental meditation – i.e. the Maharishi Mahesh Yogi. Ayurveda is a theory of rejuvenation therapy. The director of the London Maharishi Ayur-Ved Health Centre clinic, Dr Roger Chalmers, is enthusiastic about the effects of such therapy on his 1,000 patients. While the mainstay of the treatment at the London Clinic is the Maharishi Ayur-Ved rejuvenation therapy, Pancha-karma is part of the treatment which promotes a sense of positive well-being, mental clarity, emotional stability and physical vitality.

Now, admittedly, the latter article says nothing about the New Age but, as we shall see, this is both the subtlety and the attraction of the movement. It will be the middle-aged, tired and overworked executives who will be among the thousands of people attracted to the claims of mental clarity, physical vitality and positive well-being!

No less a writer than Peterborough in the *Daily Telegraph* (20th May 1989) records the horror of the officials of the Royal Aldershot Officers Club when they discovered that they would be playing hosts to a psychic festival involving top clairvoyants, palmists and mediums over that weekend in May. Club Manager, George Macey, eventually tracked down the Director of New Age – so Peterborough describes Sue Ede – to discover whether there going to be any 'hokey-pokey'. He received the assu that, 'We do the Hiltons and all the big hotels. gentlemen clairvoyants wear suits and all the ladie nice dresses.'

When Shirley MacLaine's latest film *Madame Sousatzka* was released in London, one of our quality women's magazines carried a feature article by Pippa Sherwood. The headline read: 'She believes in reincarnation. Her decisions from lovers to lunch are directed by her own personal spirit guide. Some say she is a serious exponent of America's spiritual renaissance, others just label her eccentric.' The article continued:

She sparkles. There's a host of amethyst and crystal adorning her neck. A row of four precious studs glistens on each ear like purple caterpillars. These stones are not just idle embellishments: she practises and wears the crystallography she preaches, and finds that it works for her. It's also the first outward sign of the so-called New Age therapies with which she's involved.[1]

Shirley MacLaine is probably the best known exponent of popular New Age thinking. She will be mentioned a number of times in the pages of this book. She is concerned with 'Green issues', with 'self-healing' techniques. As she herself says in the article, 'If you see God as the energy within – the New Testament God – you'll be better off than seeing him as a vengeful, Old Testament God, and you'll respond to life in the same way. Which is why if you have the power to create disease, you will also have the power to heal it.'[2] She has pertinent views on death, sex, and relationships between men and women. As the article concludes: 'There's no denying that she's entered her own personal New Age, and that she's blooming with her new-found freedom.'

Writing for Christian college students (*Cubit*, Spring 1988), John Allan says that the New Age is very much with us: 'Aquarian festivals in town-halls all over the country, presenting a colourful mix of health foods, spiritual disciplines, occult schools and mental therapies; fringe societie in universities and colleges pursuing holistic techniques ar esoteric forms of spirituality, paranormal experiment popular success for astrologers, witches, mediums and alternative healers.'[3]

In the world of education, in Britain, we can focus attention on a series of Waldorf Schools linked with the name and reputation of Rudolf Steiner and his successors. Rudolf Steiner gathered his educational principles from a variety of sources – Christianity, as well as Eastern religions. Steiner had strange ideas about Jesus. The schools began to indoctrinate the children, with the result that very

good schools with highly-trained and committed staff produced children who got a good education, but whose
parents noticed their children degenerating spiritually. The
parents, however, could not get to the roots of the fundamental philosophy. This is one more example of the
deception and subtlety of the New Age.

When we move from the world of education to the world
of business, we shall discover hard-pressed executives who
have been invited to take part in residential courses designed to develop their inner selves. Probably unknown to
them, they are being encouraged to take part in one of *four*
different and yet linked schools of thought aiming to enhance their personality and performance by improving
their minds. They may find themselves submitting – and
surrendering – to such techniques as The Focus – a development of the Erhard Seminar Training – known as est.
Again, they may be caught up with Transcendental Meditation (TM) founded by the Guru Maharishi Mahesh Yogi –
whom we have already mentioned. Others may become
unwittingly involved with spiritism or the practice of Silva
Mind control or the Human Potential Movement associated with the Peak Performance Institute. All this will be
developed much more when we consider the New Age
claim that man can become God.

Addressing the Junior Anglican Clergy of the Diocese of
Chelmsford in Summer 1988, Sister Carol, a prominent
member of the General Synod of the Church of England,
described a recent visit to Glastonbury, where she had been
brought up as a child. She spoke of Glastonbury in the West
Country as burgeoning with 'New Age' spirituality. The
bookshops, pungent with incense, she described as full of
literature on mysticism, alternative therapies, the 'I Ching',
astrology and the occult. In a courtyard off the high street a
whole range of 'possibilities' were on sale, plus the chance
to go on a mystical tour around places where the vibes were
strong – even enter a 'miracles room'. On Chalice Well
Hill, in Chalice Well garden, one can pay an entrance fee
and join a guided tour to the well. On the well cover is a

design of integration – the Yin and the Yang – the feminine and masculine. In the garden, young people are found in meditation.

This survey makes the point that in Great Britain, and in much of Europe the New Age is springing up in a variety of subtle ways. Basilea Schlink, of the Evangelical Sisterhood of Mary in Darmstadt, Western Germany, states that the New Age movement had acquired an estimated 500,000 followers, as well as countless sympathisers, in West Germany by 1987. In America, the New Age is big business. Most bookstores will have large, clearly marked sections devoted to the New Age. In this country (in W. H. Smith's for example) you will find books under the headings of the occult, reincarnation, dreams, yoga and astrology. In America, people buy into New Age and invest in New Age institutions. There are radio stations specifically given over to the promotion of the New Age. Recent polls reveal that in the States twenty-three per cent of people believe in reincarnation, twenty-three per cent in astrology and twenty-five per cent in non-personal energy and life-force.

A further boost to the spread of the New Age movement, both in the United Kingdom and further afield, came through the repeal in 1965 of the Asian Immigration Exclusion Acts. Now for the first time since the early years of the twentieth century people from Asian and Middle Eastern countries had the same immigration rights as Europeans. This had disadvantages as well as advantages. Not only were people from the East able to share fully in the life of the West, but the trickle of Asian and Eastern religious teachers became a stream. The last days of the 1960s saw the launching of a major missionary thrust by the Eastern religions to the West, including the mobilisation of 2,000 Muslim missionaries to 'evangelise' the West.[4]

What is the New Age?

So what is this New Age? It is far easier to describe than to define. Various metaphors may help us. It is like an umbrella under which much religious truth shelters. It is an inclusive and syncretistic movement, tolerant of all except the exclusive and distinctive claims of both the Jewish and Christian revelations. It can be likened to a religious octopus whose tentacles reach out to all who attempt to satisfy the spiritual needs of men. It is a rag-bag embracing the cults, the occult, Hinduism, freemasonry, theosophy and astrology, among other movements.

It can be likened to a strongly-flowing river of thought into which various streams have flowed – for example, the streams of different Eastern religions, though some of the adherents of such would deny this. Therein lies one of the frustrations and fascinations of the New Age movement: the different component members and parts will at the same time agree with each other on such issues as concern for the preservation of this world – the green ticket – and then be diametrically opposed to each other on certain spiritual aspects.

The practices of the New Age movement will vary from those clearly forbidden in the Bible – such as spiritism and various forms of divination – to those that are morally objectionable, such as abusive and manipulative psychological techniques, to still others that seem acceptable and even desirable. As an example of the latter, there are various forms of body therapy and massage available. Massage in itself can be most beneficial, but when the masseur gives a blow-by-blow account of what he or she does and talks about manipulating deep tissues to realign the energy of your aura, you must wonder what you have let yourself in for.

The definition I like best likens the New Age to: 'A Smörgåsbord of spiritual substitutes for Christianity, all heralding our unlimited potential to transform ourselves and the planet so that a "New Age of peace, light and love will break forth"'.[5]

In a world of violence, high interest rates, economic uncertainty and growing addiction of one form or another, it is surely most attractive to think, plan and work towards a world transformed by peace, light and love. Such is the prayer of students of the New Age, and especially the disciples of Alice Bailey (1880–1949), one of the early advocates of the Theosophy Society, founded in 1875, a forerunner of New Age thinking.

Alice Bailey writes about 'The Plan'. She visualises there being one world with a one world teacher and 'avatar'. The Hindu faith speaks of the 'avatar' as a 'god' who comes down to earth in bodily form. On the surface this may sound similar to the idea of the Christian Incarnation but, as Christians will testify, its real nature is quite different. This 'avatar' will be the catalyst to bring about the New Age. To that end countless thousands of copies of the prayer, 'The Great Invocation', which calls for this avatar's appearance, have been circulated. It is a prayer frequently heard in New Age gatherings:

> From the point of light within the mind of God
> Let light stream forth into the minds of men.
> Let light descend on Earth.
>
> From the point of Love within the heart of God
> Let love stream forth into the hearts of men.
> May Christ return to Earth.
>
> From the centre where the will of God is known
> Let purpose guide the little wills of men –
> The purpose which the Masters know and serve.
>
> From the centre which we call the race of men
> Let the Plan of Love and Light work out.
> And may it seal the door where evil dwells.
>
> Let Light and Love and Power restore the Plan to Earth.[6]

The New Age appears to be primarily concerned with thought, attitudes and world issues, rather than being foremost an action-packed programme of political and social reform, though, inevitably, the two will be linked. New Agers are concerned with such issues as the horror of the nuclear holocaust, world hunger, world peace, the conservation of the physical world and its natural resources.

The worldwide concern for the future of the earth and its resources has been expressed by many. Let me quote from the 1989 Nobel Peace prize-winner, the Dalai Lama of Tibet. Speaking at 'A Global Conference of Spiritual and Parliamentary Leaders on Human Survival', in Oxford in April 1988, the Dalai Lama said:

> Sadly, though we all seek a secure future, we find ourselves confronted by many problems. The delicate balance of the earth's ecology is being eroded on the land, sea and in the atmosphere. Global population is increasing while our resources are rapidly being depleted. The awesome spectre of nuclear annihilation looms over us all. If the present generation does not find some means to solve these problems, future generations may not be able to cope with them . . . Although previous generations could not claim the degree of development we have achieved, at least the world they bequeathed to us was intact. Never, in the history of humankind, has a generation been capable of producing global extinction. It is time to examine ourselves and correct where we've gone wrong.

These are matters that concern everyone; we share a common responsibility for our world regardless of our beliefs. But uniting on one front does not by any means remove all difference between us. Just as Christians will agree with the Dalai Lama on this but may disagree on plenty of other issues, so likewise our attitude to New Agers who share this concern for the world will be very mixed.

New Agers, like Christians, are concerned with the future. Both will show a firmly-based confidence in the future of the world and of mankind but there the similarity ends – for the reasoning and assumptions behind that thinking will differ profoundly. As we shall see later, the attractive flower of the New Age has sprung from poisonous roots.

The Roots of the New Age

I have already mentioned that there are several strands of thought that have influenced the New Age movement. I want to expand a little more on each so that when we understand where the New Age has come from, we shall more fully understand what it is. (The next chapter will cover this subject in more detail.)

1. The Age of Aquarius

First, in both the States and Britain, it has sprung from the Age of Aquarius and the 'counter-culture' of the 1960s. It is thought that sometime in the 1970s we passed from the astrological age of Pisces – the Fish – into the Age of Aquarius – the Water-Bearer. The Age of Pisces stretched back to the beginning of Christianity and therefore covered the Reformation, the Renaissance, and the age that gave rise to humanism. The Age of Pisces was seen as the age of authority. Everything was black and white. It was the time when the Judaeo-Christian religion was dominant and controlled man's thinking. Now, say proponents of the New Age – like Marilyn Ferguson in her book *The Aquarian Conspiracy* (1980)[7] – is the time to cast off this crippling system of religious thought.

Marilyn Ferguson's thesis is that approximately every 2,000 years there is a purely astronomical shifting of the vernal equinox through a new constellation of the zodiac. This is thought to affect the fate of planet earth. New Agers are not agreed about the exact time when the Age of Aquarius will begin. Some teach, as we have seen, that the Age of Pisces has already passed, and the Age of Aquarius has, therefore, begun. Others, like Marilyn Ferguson believe that at the turn of this century the vernal equinox will pass from the constellation of Pisces (The Fishes) to the constellation of Aquarius (The Water-Bearer). The Fish was the sign taken by the early Church to signify their faith in Jesus Christ. The so-called 'Aquarian Conspiracy' sees that age passing away, and the Water-Bearer (being a symbol of water poured out over the earth) heralding the coming of a new spirit. Through such techniques as yoga and meditation this spirit will lead the people to 'conscious expansion' in the advent of the New Age.

2. Eastern religion and belief

The second strand is that of Eastern religion and belief. This includes – Zen Buddhism, yoga, *Karma*, reincarnation, self-realisation, and TM. Basic to Hinduism and Buddhism is the notion of Oneness – All is One – monism. Thus a man, a rock or a plant might to the human eye be very different, but to the human mind and understanding they are one. They are one because All is God (pantheism). God is not a separate person; God is spirit and everywhere. Thus we understand that humanity is God – a complete reversal of the Christian understanding of God, man and creation with all the clear distinctions contained in the account of creation in Genesis 1 and 2. Man, therefore, needs to become conscious of the god that is within him, and of the potential that he possesses. Since All is One (monism), and All is God (pantheism), and humanity is God, it follows that all religions are one. What could be more attractive than this in the multi-faith, multi-racial and multi-cultural society in which most of us live. We find the barriers between our fellow men breaking down. There is an optimism based on the idea of world evolution both in this life and in the life to come.

3. The world of the occult

The third strand is related to the world of the occult, with its various manifestations of tarot cards, Ouija boards, mediums, seances, white witches and spirits of one kind or another. This strand of the New Age reflects the redis-covered awareness of the supernatural, following the sterile period when humanism reigned supreme. Christians might be encouraged that New Agers acknowledge the reality of the spirit world and the supernatural. Sadly, New Agers don't understand the same reality as Christians do by these terms.

Doctrine, Terminology and Symbolism of the New Age

New Agers reject the basic orthodox beliefs of the Christian Church. They discard the absolute values and standards of the Bible. To them, God is dead; the Bible is just another book; all truth is relative. It is as if, having discovered a gulf between themselves and the supernatural reality which they believe exists, they rushed out and produced a ladder by which to ascend to the truth. Sadly, for them, the ladder has faulty rungs; some essential rungs are missing, and they are left trying to climb to ultimate reality using the rickety ladder of man's finite understanding. They have kicked away the Christian ladder of God's ultimate truth with its safe rungs of God's revelation in the Bible, and of Jesus.

It is tragic to substitute the wobbly ladder of man's making in place of the salvation which God has provided. It is even more tragic to give the substitute and all its parts the same names and terminology as the Christian does, as if to pretend they are one and the same.

The New Age consistently teaches that a personal god does not exist, that Jesus is not the only begotten Son of God, and is not *the* Christ. It teaches that Jesus did not die for our sin, because there are no such realities as sin and evil and death. It denies the Trinity of the Father, the Son and the Holy Spirit. It asserts that the Bible is full of errors, that there is no heaven or hell, and that every man is a god, and one's godhead can be realised through the attainment of a higher consciousness.

In spite of this, the New Ager will speak in terms of the kingdom of God, the Messiah, and other expressions that are familiar to the Christian.

An example of this confusion and deception is the use of the rainbow as the most common symbol of the New Age movement. To the Christian, the rainbow (mentioned in Genesis 9:13–16; Ezekiel 1:28; and Revelation 4:3, 10:1) speaks of the promise of God never to destroy the world; of his mercy to a sinful, disobedient world; of his faithfulness to Noah leading to his covenant relationship in which he will be our God, and we shall be his people. When we see the rainbow in the sky after rain, it reminds us that God will be faithful to his promises to all generations. It reminds us (especially in the references in the Book of Revelation) of God's salvation and forgiveness for sinners, made possible through the death of Jesus upon the cross. It reminds us that we can have confidence about the future because God is enthroned on high in heaven. For the Christian the rainbow testifies to practically every one of the tenets of faith that New Agers reject.

To the New Ager, however, the symbol of the rainbow has a very different meaning. Firstly, it is regarded as the 'An tankarana', the link between the soul of men and Lucifer. This idea has been taken over from the occult tradition of the American Indians. Secondly, the rainbow, with its rays, is used as the symbol to identify one with another and to express a bond of unity between the different groups which make up its network. Thirdly, it is used as a means of meditation linked with a numerology of the occult rays. Mrs Constance Cumbey, in her book *The Hidden Dangers of the Rainbow*,[8] states that 'six' is the number of manifestation. To someone claiming to manifest the Christ consciousness, which is what the Antichrist will do, using the number six would indicate that he claimed this quality.

Now we need to acknowledge that we may see rainbows on stationery, tee-shirts, the fronts of shops and trade catalogues, and we must not assume that every time we see the rainbow we are handling something from the New Age. However, we must realise that for the New Ager, the rainbow is an especially powerful symbol. Such is the simplicity, boldness and deception of the New Age movement.

Discerning New Age Teaching and Influence

If we can be hoodwinked by the terms that the New Age uses, how can we become aware of its teaching and pervasive influence? One obvious answer is through some of the recognised, standard books of the movement. We have already noted the writings of people like Alice Bailey, and Marilyn Ferguson. To be added to this list are Fritjof Capra's book – *The Turning Point* (1982)[9] and David Spangler's *The Rebirth of the Sacred* (1984).[10] Fritjof Capra's book takes as its basic thesis the idea that history is not the story of humanity's fall into *sin*, and its *restoration* by God's saving acts. Rather, history is the story of humanity's fall into *ignorance* and the gradual climb upwards into *enlightenment*.

David Spangler is a prominent New Age leader, and for three years was the co-director of the Findhorn Foundation in Scotland which he joined in 1970. His early writings, published by Findhorn, were difficult to understand. However, his main thinking may be summed up as follows: 'Lucifer works within each of us to bring us to wholeness, and as we move into a new age, which is the age of man's wholeness, each of us in some way is brought to that point which I term the Luciferic initiation, the particular doorway through which the individual must pass if he is to come fully into the presence of his light and his wholeness.'[11]

Another way we can recognise New Age influences is to be aware of the vocabulary the movement adopts, the political concerns it embraces and the practices it follows. For example, the 1989 political Conference of the Green Party in Britain began with a few minutes' silence so that delegates could get in touch with their inner selves. Is the Green Party New Age? There appear to be some significant practices and suggestive terms used. Yet I am persuaded that no political party is explicitly New Age and that the majority of party members would not understand what the issues were. I am equally persuaded that a substantial number of individual members would firmly refute the teachings of New Age, and hold to traditional Christian teaching, values and practices. However, some individual supporters may well consciously adopt the thinking of New Age.

Therein lies the problem for most of us. None of these three guidelines – the vocabulary used, the concerns involved or the practices adopted – are by themselves conclusive and definitive. At best we can only say they serve as warning lights.

At the heart of the New Age lies the conviction that humanity is poised between two ages. Man is at the crossroads between the age of Pisces with its traditional values, standards and beliefs of the Judaeo-Christian era, and the emerging Age of Aquarius, in which he believes himself freed from the constraints of abstaining from evil, and the authoritarianism of the old order.

The decision that we make now – as communities, nations and individuals – will be crucial for the rest of our lives, and for the future of the world. Should we embrace the teaching, aspirations and philosophy of the New Age movement and its component groups, or should we examine or re-examine for ourselves the historic teaching, claims and demands of the Christian faith, and of Jesus Christ? The rest of this book helps us in that examination and decision.

2

The Origins of the New Age

We are now in the post-Christian Age of Aquarius: a new age has dawned. Or so we are told. In one sense I agree: Western society is post-Christian and wide open to new religious ideas.

One man wrote to a newspaper mistakenly accusing me of failing 'to analyse the attractions of meditation, hypnosis or the occult.' He rightly observed, however, that 'One reason is that people seek for any relief against the alienation and desolation of modern consumerism.'[1]

Marilyn Ferguson refers to similar remarks from Zbigniew Brzezinski, Chairman of the United States Security Council. She says he 'spoke of an "increasing yearning for something spiritual" in advanced Western societies where materialism has proven unsatisfying. People are discovering . . . that 5 per cent per annum more goods is not the definition of happiness. *Traditional* religion . . . does not provide a substitute: "This is why there is a search for personal religion, for direct connection with the spiritual . . ."'[2]

This post-Christian spiritual vacuum provides fertile soil for the seeds of New Age thinking. And the Church is, of course, largely responsible for our being in a post-Christian society. Many people's experience of church is of being sent to Sunday School or services each week. The services seemed (were?) boring and irrelevant. The media presentation of church and clergy reinforces this thoroughly unattractive image.

The stiff-upper-lip characteristic of English religion is

suspicious of religious experience. Through the years it has
resisted such direct experience of God. Two hundred years
ago John Wesley, the founder of Methodism, stressed a
direct experience of God through faith in Christ. Bishop
Butler wrote to him, 'Sir, the pretending to extraordinary
revelations and gifts of the Holy Ghost is a horrid thing; yes
sir, it is *a very horrid thing*.'[3]

With this strong unemotional influence in Western religion it is little wonder that people are turning to New Age
techniques and 'direct connection with the spiritual'. And
this is terribly frustrating to many Christians. On the one
hand we know that there is a deep and immensely satis-
fying spiritual experience available to those who make a
commitment by faith to Jesus Christ. And we know that
many churches are helping people into such a commitment.
Many churches too demonstrate the power of God in other
ways, such as healing. Yet this is rarely portrayed in
unbiased form by the media.

On the other hand we know that whereas involvement in
New Age techniques can lead to a superficial happiness,
rather like a spiritual drug trip, it has also led to fear,
breakdown and even suicide.

The Influence of Oriental Religions

It is into this post-Christian spiritual vacuum that the
growing influence of Eastern religion has come in recent
decades. In fact such influence goes back a long way. The
British Empire covered much of the oriental world and
brought many Westerners into direct contact with the
religious views of the East. Originally it merely produced a
fascination with these ideas. But with the waning of Christianity in the twentieth century oriental religious views
have become more acceptable. The widespread interest in
ideas such as reincarnation illustrates this point. Of course,
the huge numbers of immigrants from the East has helped
this process.

Then came the Beatles who popularised Hinduism in the 1960s. One of their biographers wrote:

> When John Lennon first met Paul McCartney their encounter in the late fifties led to events which shook the world. That is no exaggeration. How many of us can look around and deny that the Beatles at least *seemed* to initiate many of those changes in our social attitudes and tastes that took place in the sixties and which still reverberate today? Possibly it was just good luck to be so closely identified with these mass changes in consciousness.[4]

In 1966 George Harrison discovered Eastern mysticism and subsequently devoted himself to it. In February 1967 he first made contact with the Maharishi Mahesh Yogi. He said,

> I realize now that it was the spiritual side of Indian music which attracted me in the first place. Now it is the only reason for living. The reason for being here is to have a full understanding of the spiritual aspects of life. Eastern religion taught me that the ideal is to become one with God through meditation and Yoga.[5]

Later in the year the other Beatles met up with the Maharishi and then in the spring of 1968 spent some time with him in India. Commenting on the record 'Living in the Material World' released by Harrison in 1973, the same biographer says,

> It is not the function of this book to comment on George Harrison's religious beliefs – so long as Harrison himself can refrain from didactically imposing said Holy Memoirs upon innocent record-collectors. Unfortunately that is what he did (to excess) on this LP, and, therefore, it seems fair to point out that Harrison's highly publicized beliefs seem to have brought him little joy . . .[6]

Numerous other rock groups have followed the Beatles in promoting Eastern religious ideas. Their influence and

the powerful medium of rock music has conditioned
thousands of Westerners at least to begin to embrace
those ideas. And they are fundamental to New Age
thinking.

A Concern for World Peace and Harmony

We have noted that immigration has contributed to the
acceptance of oriental religious ideas in the West. But there
is another important aspect which has further encouraged
this process. With immigration has come racial tension and
confrontation. This has become a major problem in recent
decades. In the last few years there has been a growing
attempt to foster contact and understanding between the
different faiths in order to combat racism. Not only are
some church groups encouraging this but also some secular
groups. For example, the Greater London Council
mounted a campaign entitled, 'All Faiths – London Against
Racism'. One leaflet encourages people to 'organize a visit
to another religious group to learn from their faith . . .
organize a local Festival of Faith . . . hold an interfaith
service'.
    Similarly, the experience this century of two horrific
world wars followed by four decades of living on a nuclear
time-bomb has vastly strengthened the peace movement.
Glasnost, perestroika and the fall of the Iron Curtain has
made the nuclear threat seem remote. But that is a new
factor. Throughout the last forty years the threat has
seemed all too real. And this had led increasingly to
inter-faith co-operation to achieve peace and harmony
throughout the world. For example, there is the World
Conference on Religion and Peace which organises the
annual Week of Prayer for World Peace, drawing together
at least ten of the world's religions. Another group is Prayer
for Peace which encourages people around the world to
pray for peace for one minute at noon. The prayer used is of
Hindu origin. On 27th October 1986 Pope John Paul II

called leaders of the world religions together at Assisi to pray for peace.

However laudable the motives for such activities may seem, they are making a major contribution to the spread of the oriental religious ideas which are the basis of New Age thinking.

But the New Agers go further. They realise that in order to bring peace one has got to deal with the problem of human nature. 'At this point in human evolution there can be no way out of the global political stalemate unless there is first, and fast, a new humanity with a changed psychology. That new psychology is developing, a new humanity is emerging.'[7] 'You cannot make the world non-violent and loving unless you make yourself non-violent and loving.'[8]

Many Christians know that human nature can be radically transformed for the better through a faith commitment to Jesus Christ. But this truth has been lost in all too many churches. They have degenerated into religious clubs for people who like or feel the need for religious observance. Little wonder that people are turning to the transforming techniques of the New Age movement which will lead them away from God and into the occult. Once again the failure of many (not all) churches contributes to the rise of the New Age movement.

Concern for Conservation

We shall return to this subject in some depth later. But suffice it to say here that the recent explosion of concern about 'Green' issues has helped forward New Age thinking. One current but very misleading idea is that the hitherto dominant Judaeo-Christian religious tradition in the West has led to an exploitation of nature. We are told that what is needed is the respect for nature shown in Hinduism and that only such a religious idea will give sufficient foundation for the radical changes needed to save the planet. There is a very fine line between concern for ecology and an earth mysticism based on oriental (New Age) religious concepts.

The New Physics and Biology

Marilyn Ferguson describes the mysterious world which physicists are discovering: the sub-atomic world is vastly different from the world as we normally experience it; the physical laws in this sub-atomic world of quantum physics are quite different from the laws of nature as we know them:

> Matter has only 'a tendency to exist'. There are no things, only connections. Only relationships . . . In place of a real and solid world, theoretical physics offers us a flickering web of events, relationships, potentialities. Particles make sudden transitions, 'quantum leaps', behaving at times like units, yet mysteriously wave-like on other occasions.[9]

Ferguson describes this mysterious sub-atomic world as 'like Shiva's dance in Hindu mythology'.[10] She continues: normally, 'our brains mathematically construct "hard" reality by interpreting frequencies from a dimension transcending time and space'.[11] But the real world is actually this latter mysterious dimension. And, 'transcendental experiences – mystical states – may allow us occasional direct access to that realm. Certainly, subjective reports from such states often sound like descriptions of quantum reality, a coincidence that has led several physicists to speculate similarly.'[12]

In other words, Marilyn Ferguson is arguing that the mysterious, sub-atomic, quantum world discovered by the physicists is the same world that the mystics (and New Agers) have been experiencing through meditation or mystical states. She is claiming that it is scientific proof of the validity of such experiences. This is a real encouragement for New Age thinking and many people will be influenced by reading such things to pursue New Age experiences.

Ferguson also reports the advances in evolutionary thinking in biology. She points out that, 'Darwin's theory of evolution by chance mutation and survival of the fittest has proven hopelessly inadequate to account for a great many observations in biology.'[13] She believes that there are too many gaps and too many missing links for Darwin's theory to be true; also that it is no longer credible to argue that the reason for this is that the fossil record is inadequate. So, she explains, a new theory has been put forward called Punctuationalism or punctuated equilibria. Basically, this means that the smooth progress (or equilibrium) of life is punctuated from time to time by severe stress. This stress may be caused by individuals from a particular species being isolated from their fellows.

So evolution can happen in sudden 'bursts' caused by stress. Marilyn Ferguson believes that mankind is on the verge of a sudden evolutionary leap forward caused by the stress experienced by those who are pioneers on the psycho-spiritual frontiers of human experience. So through meditation and other New Age techniques people will experience a quantum leap in evolution to a new level of consciousness, an awareness of the real world behind appearances. This type of thinking is attractive to many modern Westerners.

She concludes that:

the discoveries of science have begun to make sense of mystical experiences people have been describing for millennia. They suggest that we can tap into that order of reality *behind* the world of appearances . . . We can have access to a wider sensory realm and the mystical dimension by altering the brain's biochemistry. Meditation, breathing exercises, and fasting are among the common techniques for shifting brain function.[14]

Dissatisfaction with Orthodox Medicine

There has been a revolution in Western thinking about medicine in recent years. Gone is the sole reliance on orthodox methods like drug therapy. The gap between this and 'alternative medicine' is rapidly being bridged. There is a reaction against the sometimes rather impersonal and compartmentalised approach of the medical profession. Holistic medicine is growing in popularity because it treats the whole person, physically and psychologically, not just the diseased part.

This trend has created an openness to the new healing techniques which have entered the West alongside the oriental religious influences we have already noted. In fact, many of these alternative therapies are based on oriental religious and mystical techniques.

Marilyn Ferguson notes:

> No one had realized how vulnerable the old medical model was. Within a few short years, without a shot being fired, the concept of holistic health has been legitimized by American federal and state programs, endorsed by politicians, urged and underwritten by insurance companies, coopted in terminology (if not always in practice) by many physicians, and adopted by medical students.[15]

She continues: 'The proliferating holistic health centres and networks have drawn many into the consciousness movement.'[16] By this she means the New Age movement which seeks to transform human consciousness by various techniques based on oriental religious views and occultism.

Perhaps the best known healing technique Ferguson refers to is acupuncture. She states that, 'the image of the body as a responsive field of energy, predominant in Eastern philosophy, coincides with evidence that the acupuncture meridians [energy lines within the body] are a reality and that the chakras [centres of spiritual power in the body] of Buddhist lore may indeed have a basis in fact.'[17]

Acupuncture is based on Taoism which is concerned with achieving self-awareness through mysticism and occult practices. It is a technique for manipulating the Ch'i or life-force said to flow through the body.

The fact that people are turning to New Age healing techniques which can be spiritually damaging is an indictment of the Christian Church; clearly it has not sufficiently publicised the good news that Jesus Christ heals today, through the healing ministry of his Church. Thank God this is changing, and that there are churches in most areas which offer a healing ministry.

The Influence of the Counter-Culture and Drug Culture of the 1960s

As we have noted, the New Age movement seeks to encourage the transformation of human consciousness so that we become aware of the 'real' world, that of the mystics, which lies behind the *apparently* real world.

Many thousands of people began to experiment with psychedelic or mind-altering drugs in the 1960s. Marilyn Ferguson comments,

> It is impossible to overestimate the historic role of psychedelics as an entry point drawing people into other transformative technologies . . . Those who ingested psychedelics soon found that the historic accounts closest to their own experiences derived either from mystical literature or from the wonderland of theoretical physics . . . LSD gave a whole generation a religious experience.[18]

These drug-induced experiences have led many to try other techniques to achieve altered states of consciousness. Various forms of meditation are used widely as a means to this end:

> The individual may experience himself as a field of consciousness rather than an isolated entity. Past, present and future are

juxtaposed. Space itself seems multi-dimensional, limitless.
Matter is no longer perceived as tangible but disintegrates into
patterns of energy. Subjects report direct experience of micro-
cosm and macrocosm, vibrating molecules and spinning gal-
axies, archetypes and deities, the reliving of early experiences,
even what seems to be their own birth or uterine existence . . .
If it can be demonstrated that subjects in unusual states of
consciousness have access to accurate information about the
universe, if they experience it as portrayed by quantum-
relativistic physics, we might have to abandon the derogatory
term 'altered states of consciousness'. At least some of these
states might be seen as a valid source of information about the
nature of the universe and the dimension of the human mind.[19]

Fascination with the Paranormal

There is a growing fascination with extra-sensory perception, science fiction, fantasy role-play and the occult. Such
activities have, of course, been around for a very long time.
But they have been popularised by the mass media so that
they have been brought into the living rooms of millions of
people who at one time would never have been confronted
with such influences. The decline of even nominal Christianity has removed the traditional protections against
occult involvement. Previous generations may have been
only nominally Christian but that was enough to warn them
of the dangers and evils of the occult. And it preserved
many people from involvement in such practices.

Now, however, such restraints have largely disappeared.
With the growth of materialism and the failure of high
living standards to satisfy the spiritual needs of Westerners,
the resulting spiritual hunger has all too often been 'satisfied' with the occult. So at one time Hallowe'en was a
simple games evening. Now it is a serious enough event for
balanced professional organisations like the Association of
Christian Teachers to warn against it. Some bishops have
followed suit.

A report on exorcism commissioned by the Bishop of

Exeter in 1972 states that: 'In Western countries today, the widespread apostasy from the Christian faith, accompanied by an increasing recourse to black magic and occult practices, is revealing the presence and the power of evil forces.'[20]

A non-Christian book on witchcraft states that,

Despite the fact that superstition has always been with us, the last few years of the 1960s saw a flowering of interest in occult matters which would have been inexplicable to an earlier generation . . . Now . . . it seems scarcely possible to pick up a newspaper or turn on a television set without some reference being made to ghosts, demons, magicians or witches. The occult, which lay dormant for so many years, is once again up and thriving all around us.[21]

The Rev. John Richards (ex-Secretary of the Bishop of Exeter's Study Group on Exorcism) in a chapter entitled 'The Occult Explosion' comments:

it is ironic that the 1737 Witchcraft Act was not repealed until 1951 when the decline of rationalistic thinking had contributed to the resurgence of witchcraft once again . . . There are a multitude of social factors contributing to the contemporary rise of occultism . . . There is a boom in the occult, parapsychology, astrology and all the multitude of paraphernalia which surround them. It has become a vast industry with a turnover of millions a year . . . The technological society appears not only to cause people to react towards the mystical and the supernatural, but encourages and equips them to do so.[22]

Some people may not immediately see the connection between this growth in witchcraft, spiritualism etc. and the New Age movement. It is important to realise that there is nothing particularly new about the New Age movement except, perhaps, its terminology and subtlety. The New Agers don't talk about mediums and seances but they do speak of 'channelling', meaning the same thing. They don't speak of demonisation or even demon possession but they do speak of opening oneself up to an imaginary guide who will help one to focus on the god within. This is actually the same thing as opening oneself to demonic influence or even (at its most serious) demonic control. Part of the very danger of the New Age movement is the subtlety of its language. Although dressed up in new language New Age is plain old fashioned occultism. And modern Western society is wide open to it.

But there are other even more subtle influences helping people to be open to the New Age movement. Take, for example, the heavy science fiction emphasis in the media on human beings with special powers – some of them appearing quite innocent, others more sinister. It is all part of a widespread propaganda campaign to encourage people to look within themselves to discover (or rather open themselves to invasion by) supernormal powers. This is crucial to New Age techniques.

A Desire for Community

We live in an atomistic, mobile society. All too often there is little sense of community. The old extended family communities have broken down. A family has even been defined as a group of individuals held together by a television set! And there is no doubt that the television age has furthered the breakdown of community in favour of a rather isolated individualism.

The complexity of modern Western technological society can easily make the individual feel he is merely a set of numbers on various national computers.

John Richards comments:

> The promise of the occult is to increase man's status . . . Individuals are increasingly acting in groups, because it is in a group that they find identity. The need for identity and pur-

pose, the need to matter as an individual, is driving more and more to occult practices in the hope of having an experience which will distinguish them from their fellow-workers and fellow-commuters, and give them entry into an esoteric group in which they will have status and power.[23]

There is, of course, here an indictment of many (but not all) Christian churches. The Church is meant to provide a true community where individuals matter and find acceptance and love. All too often churches fail to do this. But, thankfully, there is usually a church in each area providing such a sense of community. It may require a search but it is well worth the effort.

The Influence of Evolutionary Philosophy

Evolutionary theory has encouraged an optimism about human development. In simple terms, humanity is said to be progressing up the evolutionary scale. And this very pervasive thinking is conditioning modern man to accept the idea of spiritual evolution. We touched on this in the earlier section on the New Physics and Biology.

Marilyn Ferguson writes, 'Contemporary mystical experiences from many individuals and many parts of the world have centred in recent years on a collective and intensifying vision, the sense of an impending transition in the human story: an evolution of consciousness as significant as any step in the long chain of our biological evolution.'[24]

'Is it possible,' she asks, 'that we . . . are expressing a collective need, preparing for an evolutionary leap?' Physicist John Platt has proposed that humankind is now experiencing an evolutionary shockfront and 'may emerge very quickly into co-ordinated forms such as it has never known before . . . implicit in the biological material all along, as surely as the butterfly is implicit in the caterpillar.'[25]

Sir George Trevelyan, founder of the Wrekin Trust, a New Age organisation, says,

> In spiritual and even physical terms something is happening which is polarising humanity into two different levels. There are those who are lifting to the light and are being prepared to set aside ego, will and desire and who are taking part in dedicating life to wholeness, and there are those who, through free will, are stopping it happen.[26]

Trevelyan suggests that humanity is coming to the end of the rationalist–materialist age; the prevailing chaos and tumult is but a cleansing preparatory to the dawn of a new golden era. We are witnessing the emergence of a new human species, embodying male and female sensibilities – *Mulier Homo Sapiens Noeticus* – a human directed by consciousness, dedicated to building a society based on 'seizing the possibility of a new form of knowledge'.[27]

Conclusion

The New Age movement is an idea whose time has come. It appears to fit so neatly into the needs and aspirations of modern Western society. But behind its wholesome, exciting, fulfilling veneer are occult influences. Promising fulfilment, it unleashes forces the individual cannot control. For some who remain committed New Agers the delusion may continue for life. For others, especially those deeply involved, who try to withdraw from New Age activities, the harsh reality will dawn. They will realise that they are hooked and the withdrawal symptoms are horrific.

3

Man Becomes God

'Thou hast made us for Thyself, and our hearts are restless until they find their rest in Thee.'[1] Such is the famous prayer and longing of St Augustine of Hippo. Augustine, as a young man, indulged in most of the sexual vices and immoral physical habits possible. He was seeking fulfilment. His mother Monica prayed to God for her son's conversion to Christianity. God answered those prayers. Augustine became one of the great thinkers, leaders and saints of the Western Church.

His experience illustrates the fact that man first seeks personal fulfilment; that he may then seek fulfilment in a variety of ways that do not satisfy; and, thirdly, that lasting and spiritual fulfilment is found in God alone.

The New Age movement reflects the first two of these facts. With the rediscovery of the spiritual, New Age seeks to find God. It teaches and practises that God is found in everyone, and that as man fulfils his potential – through a variety of means – he becomes God. It is the evidence, experience and effectiveness of that hope which we now want to examine.

Developing Man's Potential

A cartoon in the appointments section of the *Sunday Telegraph* (8th October 1989) showed a man on a pedestal, exalted above his fellow men, looking down at their up-turned faces. Out of his mouth and mind came the words,

'What do I want in life? . . . a coat would be nice.' One of those looking up replies, 'Think positive, man . . . go for a three-piece suit.' Alongside the picture Geoffrey Tyrrell reports: 'Everyone has the feeling that he wants to achieve more – but how to put this into practice is another matter.' 'New Age' thinking is a concept designed to unlock this potential. The key to its success lies in the exhortation: 'That which you can conceive and believe in, you can achieve.' The article goes on to report that many business companies – including the giant complex of ICI – are training their staff in the techniques of this concept to enhance positive attitudes and success at work. What hard-pressed business men and women will find themselves involved in will be one of four different, yet linked, schools of thought aiming to enhance their personalities and per-formance by changing their minds. Among the most common methods are:

(i) The Focus – a development of the Erhard Seminar Training, formerly known as est.

(ii) Transcendental Meditation (TM) founded by the Guru Maharishi Mahesh Yogi.

(iii) Silva Mind control.

(iv) (and the Human Potential Movement associated with) the Peak Performance Institute.

An est weekend, for instance, is based on a series of related exercises. The secret of success is to allow one's mind to go blank, to empty it of all thought. The leader of the weekend then leads the participants through various stages of enlightenment, so that the delegate feels that he is on the way to becoming God.

Two examples from satisfied customers will bear this out: 'The Yes to Success programme couldn't have come at a better time for me,' one student is quoted. 'I was moving and planned to rent a room in someone's house. It made me ask myself what I really wanted. The answer was clear and simple, to have a house of my own. I found a house, and despite being a student with no full time income, was able to arrange a mortgage.'

A second customer – a personnel manager at Volvo – reported: 'Of all the techniques I have tried, TM is the most attractive because it is so simple and the results so profound and apparent after a short time of practice. My ability to concentrate has increased. I find solutions to problems much more quickly' (quoted in the *Sunday Telegraph*, 8th October 1989).

It was estimated in about 1986 that some 500,000 people had had such experiences, including world-famous people like Yoko Ono and John Denver. Again, the *Sunday Telegraph* article states that fifty per cent of the 1,200 employees at ICI Engineering are estimated to have attended such courses. One employee is quoted as saying that after attending a course his attitude to things going wrong had changed. Instead of thinking: 'This is just like me,' he says, 'I now look at the positive side. Things get better and I feel happier, which produces better results.'

While we have mentioned four main groups or techniques for changing one's attitude and developing self-fulfilment, the variety within each seems almost without limit. A three-page review of the New Age scene in London (*Options*, November 1989) acknowledges the impossibility of doing justice to the full range of therapies and groups available but, under a section headed 'Mind', lists the following (with contact names and addresses): psychotherapy, assertion training, life skills, sexual therapy, metanoia, Gestalt, hypnotherapy, and soul-directed therapy.[2] The overlap and the confusion that abounds for the individual seeking what is helpful and what is harmful is clear from such a list. The ultimate objective of each path would, nevertheless, be similar – to help people to find self-fulfilment, and to be in charge of their lives and master of their own souls.

Shirley MacLaine, perhaps the best known advocate of the New Age movement, would agree with this. She has endeared herself to her massive public around the world through her films, TV series and books. All the while she was searching for identity. (It is interesting that during this period she is not aware of meeting any committed Christians who could have helped her.) She affirms that nothing is more powerful than the collective human mind. Douglas Groothuis sums up her essential message as contained in four stages. First, each person is a god (although they might be ignorant of it). Second, each one has lived before and will live again; third, there is no death, and lastly, there are as many realities as there are people since we create our own reality.[3]

The actress seeks to be in contact with 'beings' from the other side. She is an avid follower of Ramtha, reputedly a 35,000-year-old ascended master who conveys his messages through the author J. Z. Knight. Ramtha would teach that God, '. . . has never been outside of you . . . it is you . . . God, of itself, is wholly without goodness or evil . . . God simply is.'

The subtle dangers of this New Age teaching are not limited to beautiful actresses and overworked businessmen and women. Children can subconsciously become caught up in its thinking. For example, Luke Skywalker from the Star Wars saga can unwittingly lead children down the wrong pathway. George Walker, the creator of the series, has Luke Skywalker initiated into the league of Jedi knights; this involves mastering the 'force' that animates the cosmos, dwells within and is tapped intuitively through feelings. Millions of young minds will be familiar with the 'force', and the desire for ability to control the world.

The New Age influence is found even in the classroom. One Los Angeles teacher invited her class of twenty-five primary schoolchildren to imagine that they were doing something perfect, and that they were perfect. The children were taught to see themselves as resplendent with light, and to be at peace, for they were perfect. They were reminded that they had within themselves all the wisdom of the universe.[4]

Thus the evidence of man striving to become God is quite

clear, but we need to examine the basic thinking behind these ideas and concepts to understand them more clearly.

The Thinking Behind 'Man Becomes God'

There are some basic technical terms we have to grasp if we are to understand New Age thinking. One of these is the term 'Monism'. Man and god and everything that is created are one. There are no distinctions between a person, a plant, a planet and a paper-bag. Even more importantly, New Age thinking blurs the essential distinctions between male and female. The movement seeks to dethrone man, and exalt women. It campaigns against the overemphasis of the masculine principle. It wants to abolish rational, analytical thinking and to eliminate the inequalities between the sexes. The ultimate aim is the dominance of the female principle which supposedly corresponds to the spirit of the Age of Aquarius.

One manifestation of this female domination, and the dethroning of God as creator, is the reference to the earth as Mother Earth, and nature as Mother Nature. For example, the final prayer in the section 'A Call to Reconciliation' at the Festival of Faith held in Canterbury Cathedral in September 1989 was addressed to Mother Nature. It stated, 'We are here, our brothers and sisters of the creation, with your life in our hands and your cries ringing in our ears. We who are part of you have set ourselves apart from you.'

Such a prayer lends support to the Christian claim that the God who is revealed in the Bible as our creator and maker has been rejected by New Age teaching (as well as by many others).

All this is consistent with the basic tenets of the New Age. Monism tells us that All is One. Pantheism teaches us that All is God. The logical result is that humanity is God. We might assume that such pantheistic thinking is only to be found on the fringes of Western society. However, C. S.

Lewis in his book *Miracles* wrote about pantheism as follows:

> Pantheism is congenial to our minds not because it is the final stage in a slow process of enlightenment, but because it is almost as old as we are . . . It is immemorial in India. The Greeks rose above it only at their peak, in the thought of Plato and Aristotle; their successors lapsed into the great Pantheistic system of the Stoics. Modern Europe escaped it only while she remained predominantly Christian; with Giordano Bruno and Spinoza it returned. With Hegel it became almost the agreed philosophy of highly educated people, while the more popular Pantheism of Wordsworth, Carlyle and Emerson conveyed the same doctrine to those on a slightly lower cultural level. So far from being the final religious refinement, Pantheism is in fact the permanent natural bent of the human mind . . . It is the attitude into which the human mind automatically falls when left to itself.[5]

And man has been left to himself. It has been said, 'Secular man killed a God in whom he could not believe, but whose absence he could not bear.' He was tired of the emptiness of secular humanism. Something has to fill the vacuum. The result was a concoction of pantheism, and a new modern psychology. Through the writings of Freud, Jung, Reich and B. F. Skinner the human potential movement emerged.

Key Influences in the Development of Modern Psychology

Sigmund Freud (1856–1939) took a psychoanalytical view of man. Freud taught that man was driven by the unconscious within and not the reason. The period of the Enlightenment was coming to a close.

Others disagreed with this Freudian view, notably Carl Jung (1875–1961) who has been termed the John the Baptist of the New Age movement. Although he was an early disciple of Freud, Jung challenged Freud's assump-

tion that all human behaviour could be reduced to and
understood in terms of sexual behaviour. He took exception also to the notion that religious beliefs were nothing
but harmful illusions. Jung was more positive than Freud.
He believed that man had a reservoir of psychological
images and forces accruing through all history and shared
by all.

William Reich (1897–1957) also challenged the Freudian
theory, but on different grounds. He believed that block-
ages to the development of the human personality were
recorded in muscular patterns in the body, forming what he
called 'character armour'. Reich developed a form of
physical touch to release the 'orgone energy' that permeated the universe. He built orgone accumulators to collect
and harness this mysterious cosmic energy. His theories
were beginning to link a psychological and philosophical
understanding of man, and this has become important to
the thinking of the New Age.

Yet another school of thought – linked with the name of
B. F. Skinner – explained human behaviour exclusively in
terms of external stimulation. Our behaviour consists of
our response to various stimuli. Skinner was to lead the way
to the Behaviourist school of thought.

Holistic Healing and Man as his own Saviour

Our brief overview of key influences in the development of
modern psychology may help us to understand two trends
that were appearing in the New Age movement. The first is
the emergence of the holistic healing movement which
claimed to give man control over his body. The second was
the emphasis upon man being his own saviour, and the
means of his own fulfilment – once he had understood what
it was that motivated him.

The holistic movement simply regarded man as a whole
being. His body, mind, spirit and will were interrelated and
interdependent. Modern Western medicine had, by and

large, reduced man to a body – the physical. It was a machine to be serviced. New Age holistic medicine, on the other hand, seeks to minister to the whole person. It might use the ancient Chinese practices of acupuncture, or the modern technique of biofeedback. It manifests itself in the local chemist or drug store with a variety of books and prescriptions, ranging from those mentioned above to self-hypnosis, meditation and macrobiotics. Through whatever means, the goal of holistic health practice is said to be that of attuning one with the One. Wherever we turn we find that man consciously or unconsciously is seeking to de-throne God as the Lord our healer, and to exalt man as capable of bringing healing to himself. Thought leads to action and behaviour. What we believe about ourselves, we shall do for ourselves. Thus modern psychology has taught people to look within themselves for answers, and not the God beyond. Theology – the study of God – is being replaced by psychology as the heart of human concern. Certainly in the States it is the 'done thing' to have your own counsellor. Man is preoccupied with self, believing that self can help him become a god.

To some readers our very sketchy overview of the history of psychological thought may be confusing. We needed to survey that territory in order to put down one or two key markers and names, and to relate a little more easily to them.

For example, Carl Jung is quoted. His teaching has been effectively, and unhelpfully, made popular among Christians by the writings of Morton Kelsey.

Christians owe a debt of gratitude to two Americans among others for exposing the error in Jung's thinking and for revealing the New Age roots of his teaching. They are Kevin Perrotta and Leanne Payne,[6] who are concerned that Christian Jungianism – and therefore Jung's basic teaching – has four weaknesses. First, there is a tendency towards self-absorption; then a tendency to confuse the self with God; thirdly, there is a tendency to confuse Jung's goal of personal completeness with the Christian goal of holiness;

finally, there is the idea that evil must be integrated rather than rejected in a person.

Jung's autobiography, *Memories, Dreams and Reflections*,[7] reveals the heart and the motivation of the Swiss psychologist. All his life he was oppressed by the demonic, by what some would call occult phenomena. Early in his life he accepted these revelations, and interpreted them to mean that God is both good and evil, that Yahweh and Satan are polar ends of one being, and that in similar fashion the psychic life has good and evil poles.

From this brief glimpse of Jung and his life, it is clear that he is a most unreliable guide and teacher. Yet he is one of the founders of the modern school of psychology that has led to the concept of Transpersonal Psychology in the New Age. This concept brings the ideas of the 'divine within' and the 'oneness of reality' (monism) into psychology. In Transpersonal Psychology the ground of all being is consciousness. As we move to a higher consciousness we shall eventually find our culmination in pure spirit. We thus become like God. It should be clear that TP (Transpersonal Psychology) embraces both Western pantheism and Eastern Hinduism and Buddhism.

This transformation of man to become God takes place through a variety of means. Among the best known are meditation and yoga, but there are four basic groups that have been identified:

  (i) Self-help training groups.
 (ii) Psychic,mind-reading,healingandprophecygroups.
(iii) Spiritism and channelling groups.
(iv) Eastern religious groups.

Mention of these last two groups reminds us again that the New Age movement takes on the guise of religious activity, with its spiritual laws and commandments, its priests and gurus, a proclaimed Messiah, and people with supernatural powers which enable them to do great signs and wonders. Repeatedly, from the Christian perspective, we come up against the subtle counterfeit of the movement and its teaching.

Sadly, this is not theory. All these ideas and notions have a practical and personal reality. *The Independent* (10th October 1989) published Simon Denison's reactions to taking part in a rebirthing weekend:

> The actual weekend, entitled 'Loving Relationships Training', was led by an American couple, Peter and Meg Kane. Rebirthing offered a superabundance of all good things with no sacrifice whatsoever. Even eternal life was promised. The central tenet of rebirthing is that thought is creative, and that our beliefs about ourselves are self-fulfilling. If we can think positively about ourselves and get rid of negative thoughts, we can eliminate our insecurities. So if a man has had an adolescent incestuous relationship with his mother and now feels guilty about close relationships with women, he is told that there is nothing wrong in loving women. He must then affirm this, over and over again, until he begins to believe this. Such approaches can even change the fact of death! The only reason we die is that we think death is inevitable. It is the biggest negative thought in the world.

It is not just 'rebirthing' that teaches that death is a myth. Another aspect of the New Age teaching is that man does not die, but is reborn into new life-cycles. The higher or lower form of reincarnation depends on how a man has lived his previous life. The automatic 'Law of Karma' remains in effect until a person perfects himself sufficiently to enter Nirvana. That is a state in which the individual ceases to exist. This is possible because the New Age states clearly that we save ourselves by finding our higher self through conscious expansion. Faith in man, and in the all-pervading energy, or life-force throughout the cosmos, is at the centre of the New Age spirituality. It is best summed up in the sentences: 'When I am, then God is gone. When I am gone, God is there.'[8]

We must not marginalise the New Age movement. J.

Gordon Melton in an article in the *Encyclopedic Handbook of Cults in America*, writes:

> The most important elements in the New Age movement are the many individuals, organisations and businesses which have arisen to facilitate the process of transformation which is at the heart of the New Age vision. Every metropolitan area has scores of individuals who teach transformation techniques from meditation to the martial arts, or who practice the various forms of alternative medicine, body therapies and psychological processes.[9]

Again, Melton attempts to measure the size and impact of the New Age movement. There is, he says, no central organisation, but there are various directories of the New Age networks. Some of these directories contain a small number of individuals and groups committed to the New Age vision. A far larger number share one or more New Age concerns (personal transformation, ecology, peace, co-operative models for living), but would not advertise themselves as primarily New Age converts and adherents. Lastly, there are many groups who as entrepreneurs provide services and products (health services, natural food products) but who may not have any personal involvement in – or even deep knowledge of – the New Age.

What is most significant in Melton's review is that New Age has been able to establish its largest constitution among single, young, upwardly-mobile, urban adults. Such people will warmly welcome the processes of transformation which must accompany career success. Thus man becomes the conscious master of his own life, and the captain of his fate. Man becomes God.

The Christian Response

How does the Christian react and respond to all this? Sometimes I expect we shall struggle to understand some of the concepts and terms which are very strange to our Western minds. We may be tempted to ignore the movement as too difficult to handle. We may even be deceived into thinking that there might be something in it, and that at least it seems to work. New Age is the child of a pragmatic age that asks, 'Does it work?' Rather we should ask the question, 'Is it true?' How does its teaching measure up to the revealed truth of God in the Bible?

At every point Christianity and the New Age are in conflict and dispute. The Christian sees God as our creator, maker, father and Sovereign over all his world and works. New Age teaches that God is within man. The New Age teaches that man's weakness is due to ignorance. The Bible states that it is due to sin. The Bible sees man as both the greatest of sinners, and also as little lower than the angels. Man's true greatness is realised when he submits himself to God. It is not realised when man reduces God to his own understanding.

Man is made in the image of God; not God made in the likeness of men. The New Age fails to acknowledge and solve the problem of sin and the provision of salvation. The New Age proclaims that man can save himself. The Bible records man's abusive shouts at Christ as he hung on the Cross: 'Aren't you the Christ? Save yourself and us' (Luke 23:39, NIV). Jesus could have saved himself. He knew that his Father could have sent ten legions of angels to deliver him. Christ *didn't* save himself, in order that he *could* completely save us.

G. K. Chesterton once said, 'When a man ceases to believe in God, he doesn't believe in nothing, he believes in anything.'[10] That is what has happened in New Age belief. Paul exposes and illustrates it in Romans 1:20 ff. In this passage he describes men as having ceased to honour and worship their creator. Instead they worship and serve creation. They are said to have exchanged the truth of God for a lie. Because of this God has given them up to the sinful desires of their hearts, to shameful lusts, to depraved minds and to do what ought not to be done.

The truth is that man cannot save himself by becoming God. Rather man can only be saved by God becoming man. That is the greater wonder and miracle, and to that we shall turn shortly. What we need to understand is that man does not need reincarnation, but regeneration. Not a higher or better life, but a new life. Man cannot be transformed by himself. He is only changed, made a new creation, and made holy by the work of Jesus Christ and the indwelling spirit of the living God.

4

New Age as Religion

One thing that attracts people to the New Age movement is that it does not appear very religious. On the face of it the movement is about wholeness, self-fulfilment, peace and ecology. But the New Age movement *is* fundamentally religious – religion being defined as belief in a higher unseen controlling power or powers; it is man's search for God which tends to project various attributes on to God. The movement is also essentially anti-Christian.

Religious Characteristics of the New Age Movement

Because the New Age movement is not characterised by obvious ecclesiastical buildings or religious services it is more difficult to demonstrate its religious nature. But certain factors are clear:

Christianity is characterised by the worshipper having a personal, loving faith relationship with God who is both transcendent (beyond ourselves, awe-inspiring) and immanent (nearby, even indwelling). Worship is an offering made with a mixture of awe and love. The individual lives his life in a way which will bring joy to God. In the words of the Shorter Catechism, 'the chief end of man' is 'to glorify God and to enjoy him for ever'. Christianity is essentially an offering to God. It fulfils what Jesus described as the first and greatest Commandment: 'Love the Lord your God with all your heart and with all your soul and with all your strength and with all your mind' (Luke 10:27, NIV).

Contrast this high, selfless ideal with the self-centred New Age religion:

1. It is a man-centred religion

One alternative name for the New Age movement is the Human Potential movement. And this indicates the essentially man-centred nature of New Age religion.

The New Age movement aims to reach the rather mystical experience of transformed consciousness for its own sake. It is not seeking an experience of God in order to worship him. Marilyn Ferguson, as a New Ager, favours the former approach. She says, 'Millennia ago humankind discovered that the brain can be teased into profound shifts of awareness. The mind can learn to view itself and its own realities in ways that seldom occur spontaneously.'[1]

She distinguishes the left hemisphere of the brain which controls rational thought, speech etc., from the right hemisphere which is more musical and sexual, thinks in images, sees in wholes and detects patterns. The latter is the so-called emotional brain. 'Meditation, chanting, and similar techniques increase the coherence and harmony in the brainwave patterns; they bring about greater synchrony between the hemispheres, which suggests that a higher order is achieved.'[2]

As we have noted earlier, this psychological manipulation can open a person to harmful supernatural influences. However, they are often well-disguised. The Bible describes Satan as an angel of light. The light conceals the evil. One person describes the effects of a form of meditation:

> Suddenly I was overwhelmed by the beauty of everything I saw. This vivid, transcendent experience tore apart my limited outlook. I had never realized the emotional heights possible. In this half-hour solitary experience I felt unity with all, universal love, connectedness. This smashing time destroyed my old reality permanently.[3]

I have had experiences I could describe in the words of the first two sentences of that quotation, in the context of praying to and meditating (in a Christian sense of quiet concentration) upon Jesus Christ. But it issued in greater worship of him. The New Agers appear to seek the experience as an end in itself. As one put it, 'we enjoy and even thrill to the god-like possibilities we see in ourselves in peak moments.'[4]

The aim of the New Age movement is deliberately to use consciousness-expanding techniques to achieve a world-wide expansion of consciousness:

> Through systematic explorations of conscious experience, using a variety of methods, they were discovering such phenomena of mind as accelerated learning, expanded awareness, the power of internal imagery for healing and problem solving, and the capacity to recover buried memories; insights from those explorations changed their values and relationships. They were reaching out now for any information that would help them make sense of their experiences.[5]

In direct contradiction to Christianity, Ferguson states, 'Human nature is neither good nor bad but open to continuous transformation and transcendence. It has only to discover itself.'[6] She sees that a Human Potential movement would help to break down the barriers between Eastern wisdom and Western action. Technology has freed us in recent decades from the struggle to survive. Before that few had the time to explore the psyche.

So the main aim of the movement is to realise the full potential of human beings. And, of course, to reach wholeness through meditation, alternative medicine, etc. Ferguson dismisses criticisms that this is narcissistic and encourages self-importance. However, it seems clear that such criticisms have a great deal of weight.

It is true that New Agers aim to encourage others to realise their potential and to make peace on earth etc. But all of this is still human-centred.

2. *It is a manipulative religion*

True Christianity is, as we have seen, to love God with our whole beings and to show that love in joyfully serving him in the supernatural power he shares with us (the power of the Holy Spirit).

By contrast, New Age religion aims to discover and use 'the god within' the individual. It shares with witchcraft and the occult the approach of seeking to manipulate the supernatural for personal ends. The fact that these may be good at times does not alter the fundamentally manipulative nature of New Age religion.

It is true that New Agers have an awareness of being part of a greater Whole. But even there it seems this greater Whole is manipulating them in a rather impersonal, pantheistic way. There is not the Christian experience of a loving inter-personal relationship with God in joyful service.

Marilyn Ferguson says,

> Beyond the personal reunification, the inner reconnection, the re-annexing of lost portions of oneself, there is the connection to an even larger Self – this invisible continent on which we all make our home . . . The separate self is an illusion . . . when the self joins the Self, there is power.[7]

She goes on to refer to the 'living, throbbing connection, the unifying I-Thou of Martin Buber, a spiritual fusion'.[8] But she clearly means by this our relationship with the collective Self – with others, not with God. 'Even beyond the collective Self, the awareness of one's linkage with others, there is a transcendent, universal Self.'[9]

There is a sense of vocation. Carl Jung defines it thus: 'Vocation acts like a law of God from which there is no escape.'[10] Ferguson comments: 'The creative person is overpowered, captive of and driven by a demon. Unless one assents to the power of the inner voice, the personality cannot evolve.'[11]

Frederick Flach put it like this: 'At the very moment

when we are struggling to sustain a sense of personal
autonomy, we are also caught up in vital forces that are
much larger than ourselves so that while we may be the
protagonists of our own lives, we are the extras or spear
carriers in some larger drama.'[12]

This all has a ring of pantheistic determinism relieved
only by the ability of the individual to manipulate the
supernatural for his own ends.

This pantheistic concept is strengthened by Marilyn
Ferguson's description of God:

> God is experienced as flow, wholeness, the infinite kaleido-
> scope of life and death, Ultimate Cause, the ground of being,
> what Alan Watts called 'the silence out of which all sound
> comes' . . . We need not postulate a purpose for this Ultimate
> Cause nor wonder who or what caused whatever Big Bang
> launched the visible universe. There is only experience. To
> Kazantzakis [the Greek novelist], God was the sum total
> of consciousness in the universe, expanding through human
> evolution. In the mystical experience there is the felt presence
> of an all-encompassing love, compassion, power.[13]

New Age Infiltration into the Church

The Church is vulnerable to New Age influence largely
because of the liberal theology popularised by people like
the Bishop of Durham. Essentially the basis of such liberal
theology is an embarrassment with the idea of the supernatural. True, proponents of liberal theology believe in
God, but they have difficulties with the concept of divine
intervention – in miracles, the virgin conception and empty
tomb, etc.

It is interesting to speculate as to where these liberals
have been whilst God has been renewing the supernatural
gifts of the Spirit (including healing and prophecy) in many
churches during the last twenty-five years.

But the liberal influence has, unfortunately, infected

many churches with an arid rationalism. Little wonder that modern man, looking for meaning, fulfilment and, perhaps often without realising it, yearning for the supernatural, regards such churches as irrelevant.

However, there is another very serious effect – on the Church itself. Liberal theology has undermined the authority of Scripture in many churches. It has also made out that some aspects of the faith – the virgin birth, the empty tomb, the miracles – traditionally held to be objective historical events, are actually mythological statements about subjective experiences. So, for example, they say it doesn't matter if Christ's tomb was empty: the resurrection stories are simply expressions of the early Christians conviction that Jesus was still spiritually present with them after the crucifixion.

So liberal theology encourages a subjective make-it-up-as-you-go-along theology. What matters, the liberals say, is not objective historic facts about Christ, but subjective experience of him. And you can choose to express it in myths, if you like.

This undermining of biblical authority means many church people do not know their Bibles. They are not taught Scripture extensively and they don't see the importance of studying it themselves. Consequently they are largely ignorant of its positive teachings and of its warnings against superstition, occult practices and heretical views of (for example) Christ. Confronted with the superstition, psycho-technologies and pseudo-Christ of the New Age movement, these people are very vulnerable. Like many non-churchgoers they are yearning for the supernatural but haven't got the safeguards provided by a knowledge of Scripture. Consequently, they get involved in New Age activity.

Even theologians are not immune. Don Cupitt, a clergyman in the Church of England, calls himself a 'Christian Buddhist'. He does not believe in an objective metaphysical God and dislikes doctrinal systems. He argues that we should become divine, find a god within, and become gods. He is a New Age theologian. The writer has given details of Cupitt's views elsewhere.[14]

One Anglican church has been described as a New Age church – St James's, Piccadilly.

St James's, Piccadilly

Marilyn Ferguson tells us that:

> an increasing number of churches and synagogues have begun to enlarge their context to include support communities for personal growth, holistic health centres, healing services, meditation workshops, consciousness altering through music, even biofeedback training.[15]

St James's is one such church. The rector, Donald Reeves, has previously sought to hinder the publication of fully-documented criticisms of his church's New Age programme. In May 1989 the magazine *Prophecy Today* accused St James's of embracing the New Age. Reeves responded in the July issue that this was:

> mischievous and misleading. It misrepresents the nature of the hospitality we have offered some parts of the New Age movement for more than seven years. It is just not true to say that we 'embrace' the New Age . . . these words give the impression . . . that we believe unconditionally all that the New Age stands for. That is not so.

He continues:

> I know of many who have found Christ through the hospitality we have offered. It is a difficult ministry, easily misunderstood and sometimes, as I have often said and freely admit, we have made mistakes. We are the only church in the United Kingdom which provides this sort of hospitality for the New Age – now worldwide, some ninety million strong.

It is clear from these statements that Donald Reeves is not denying that St James's accepts some or even much New Age thinking. He simply says it does not 'believe unconditionally all' New Age ideas. It is also necessary to ask in what sense people have found Christ. As we shall see, many New Agers speak much of the Christ but do not mean Jesus Christ, the divine–human saviour of the Bible.

Even Donald Reeves's views of Christ are unorthodox. He explains in the same article that the New Testament references to Christ as the only way of salvation are 'the language of enthusiastic believers . . . [the] language of testimony'. He continues: 'Understanding these texts about the exclusive and unique nature of Christ as confession and testimony offers freedom and opportunity to establish dialogue with other believers equally committed to their saviours, searchers and explorers of every sort.'

It is difficult to see how this squares with the statement of *Jesus himself*: 'I am the way and the truth and the life. No-one comes to the Father except through me' (John 14:6, NIV). But we shall return to this subject in the next section.

We shall now make a fully documented criticism of St James's New Age programme so that readers can assess Donald Reeves' defence for themselves. It is important to be fair in such criticisms and so it should be noted that St James's is involved in a full programme which includes lectures on socio-political subjects; concerts; workshops on prayer and spirituality; counselling facilities etc., as well as church services. Many of these events probably have nothing to do with New Age ideas.

However, it is equally true that St James's is heavily into a New Age programme which has links with the occult. This is centred on the 'Alternatives Ministry', which is described in the church's literature as being:

> concerned with what is known as New Age thinking. Essentially these are ideas which provide creative and spiritual alternatives to currently accepted Western thought . . . Alternatives is concerned with . . . Alternative Healing . . .

Ancient Wisdom . . . Earth Mysteries, Parapsychology [Psychic Research] . . . Esoteric Philosophy.[16]

It is interesting to see how many people involved with Alternatives are also involved with the Findhorn Community in Scotland. As we shall see in Chapter 6, the Findhorn Community is a leading New Age foundation. It claims to co-operate with the Devas (Hindu gods) and nature spirits who inhabit their flower and vegetable gardens. They are also co-operating with the good Pan (the Greek fertility god who is associated with pantheism). Their leaders have regularly received communications from spirit-beings, one of whom speaks of the true light of Lucifer.

It is a cause of deep concern to find that people from this foundation are leaders in St James's Alternatives programme. One director of Alternatives 'was a senior member of the Findhorn Foundation for six years, focalising the garden for two years . . . she now practises as a psychic counsellor in London and still leads workshops at Findhorn.'[17] Another director is 'closely associated with the Findhorn Foundation'.[18]

On 23rd April 1989 a Special Children's Workshop was held at St James's 'for children aged 7 to 12 years old to explore their inner and outer selves . . . Native American journeying . . . space voyage visualisations.' (These are New Age activities.) This was led by a woman who 'was instrumental in creating the youth programme at Findhorn'.[19]

Another lecture at St James's in February 1989 was by the 'chair of the Lucis Trust which operates several international programmes including the Arcane School, World Good Will and Triangles, and which publishes and distributes the teachings of Alice Bailey and the Tibetan Master, Djwahl Kuhl.'[20] Alice Bailey and the Lucis Trust are all advocates of Theosophy which is hostile to Christianity and other religions which believe in only one God. They 'deny both a personal God and personal immortality' and regard Christ as 'purely human and consequently deny the validity of the Christian Revelation'. Theosophy is a 'mixture of pantheism, magic and rationalism'[21] and blends Hindu and Buddhist ideas, particularly stressing reincarnation. Theosophists claim to be in touch with mysterious World Teachers who are incarnated in a brotherhood of Masters located in Tibet. All of this is deeply occult and anti-Christian.

This lecture was on 'The Spiritual Significance of the Full Moons' and was to 'explain how, at the time of the full moon, the energies of light, love and will-to-good are uniquely available.'[22]

On 20th April 1989, Wesak – the Buddha's Birthday – was celebrated in St James's church. The Alternatives leaflet stated:

> For many people in the new age movement, Wesak – the full moon when the sun is in Taurus – is the most important spiritual event of the year . . . There is also a living legend which states that at this full moon the Buddha and the Christ join together with all other liberated beings and with the communion of saints to invoke a great annual blessing for the planet. We shall be celebrating Wesak this year with an interdenominational meditation ceremony in the church. We invite people of all cultures, religions and belief systems to join us in this great inner celebration.[23]

Earlier in the year the Chief of the Druid Order lectured on Druidism. The ancient Druids were the religious representatives of the Celts, who worshipped a horned fertility god. Sometimes this god had as consort the 'Earth Mother'. Celtic religion included human sacrifice.

Also early in 1989 there were at St James's lectures on 'The medicine wheel teachings of the American Indians'; the importance to the 'New Age' of embodying its aspirations in dance; ley lines, 'a complex and very sensitive network of energy lines and energy centres that cover and penetrate our planet. This energy network, in turn, affects and is affected by human action.' There was another session – 'What on earth is the "New Age"?' – which focused 'particularly on the idea that humanity as a whole is entering a new form of consciousness'. This was by one of the associates of Findhorn. And there were monthly concerts of New Age music.

St James's also holds a monthly Sufi Healing Order. Sufism is an Islamic mystical movement which seeks direct experience of Allah through ascetic practices. There is also a weekly Zen Sitting (this is, of course, based on Zen Buddhism). In early 1989 there were studies of the Bhagavad Gita which features Krishna, the eighth incarnation of the Hindu god Vishnu.

The St James's, Piccadilly, programme contains a mish-mash of oriental, pagan and occult subjects. It is fertile soil for the growth of New Age ideas and influence. The fact that this is allowed in an Anglican church is, of course, a scandal of the first order. But the spineless 'tolerance' of much Anglicanism not only leaves the door open to New Age infiltration; it puts out the welcome mat. (For other information about St James's and the related New Age infiltration into the Church, see the writer's book *Our God Reigns*.)[24]

Christian compromise and inter-faith events in cathedrals

Some may be tempted to think that St James's, Piccadilly, is simply an unimportant lunatic fringe in the Church. But that would be to underestimate the context of growing inter-faith compromise in the Church. And such compromise provides a major opportunity for New Age ideas and influences to enter. It welcomes the infiltration of the very oriental religion on which the New Age movement is founded.

It is important to clarify concern about this, because the subject is easily open to misunderstanding. The problem is not one of opposition to friendly relations between people of different faiths; and there is nothing wrong with people of different faiths or none co-operating over social and moral concerns. The difficulty is of ensuring the proviso in every case that no impression be given that all religions are equally true.

It is important that in every country people have freedom of religion and conscience. One thing more: the concern about inter-faith compromise has nothing whatever to do with racism. Racism is a sin which contradicts fundamental doctrines in Christianity. There are, of course, millions of Christians in every racial group. There is no way that Christianity is a 'white religion'. One speaker at an International Conference of Anglicans asked the participants, 'What is it like to belong to a black Church?' He was pointing out that there are far more black Anglicans in the world than white.

Even in the UK there are over 84,000 members of black-led Christian churches and another 12,000 Christians of other racial groups. On the other hand, a few weeks ago national leaders within Buddhism, Hinduism and Islam in Britain, confirmed to the writer that there are many thousands of white Westerners who are involved in their religions.

No, my concern has nothing to do with race or religious freedom or friendly social or moral co-operation between religious groups. It is to do with the compromise by Christians of the Christian faith.

Briefly, the issue is this: the Bible teaches that God created man with free will and that meant freedom to choose not to obey God. Which is what man chose. The results were disastrous. Although man is created 'in the image of God' there is something seriously wrong with human nature. Every aspect of our human nature has been tainted.

So the Bible can say that, 'everyone has sinned and is far away from God's saving presence'.[25] To put it in human terms, this created a dilemma for God. On the one hand he is so loving that the Bible teaches 'God *is* love' (my italics).[26] But on the other hand he is the 'righteous Judge'[27] who will judge 'the thoughts and attitudes of the heart'[28] as well as our actions. God is light and no (spiritual) darkness can approach him.[29]

How then can man be saved? How can sinful (spiritually dark) man have access to God who is light and lives in unapproachable light?[30]

God solved this dilemma in the *only* way it could be solved. He entered the world himself and became incarnate (in-fleshed) in Jesus Christ. The Bible teaches that Jesus was both God and man.[31]

And Jesus Christ, the divine Son of God came to die. Horrific though the physical suffering of the cross was, there was worse. He cried out to his Father, 'My God, my God, why did you abandon me?'[32] He was abandoned by the Father: that means hell. The Apostle Peter explains: 'Christ himself carried our sins in his body to the cross.'[33] God himself paid the ultimate penalty for the breaking of his law. He paid the penalty we deserve. Only God could achieve such a thing but only a man could die. Hence it could only be achieved by the God-man. And without such a terrible death-penalty (spiritual as well as physical), God's just law could not be satisfied and mankind saved.

This is why Jesus is the only way of salvation. No one else was the God–man who died in this terrible way for mankind. This is not a negotiable article of faith for Christians. This is why Jesus said, 'I am the way and the truth and the life. No-one comes to the Father except through me.'[34]

The response required of mankind is a faith commitment to Jesus Christ. The Bible says that 'Christ is of no use' to those who put their trust in religious ceremonies or merely living a good life. This puts them 'outside God's grace'.[35]

Because of all this any action by Christians which states or implies that there are ways to God other than through Jesus is in serious error. If God has provided only one way of salvation, we do a great disservice to mankind (and also dishonour God) by compromising this truth.

So if non-Christian gods are worshipped on church property, or if Christians worship alongside people of other faiths, at the very least this is implying that Christians agree that there are other ways to God (or even other gods). And as we have noted, it invites the infiltration of the very oriental religion on which the New Age movement is founded.

But such inter-faith compromise is growing, even in our cathedrals. On 13th May 1984 an inter-faith service was televised from Newcastle Cathedral. This included the worship with chanting, dancing and offering of flowers of a Hindu idol. Allah was praised in a reading from the Koran. A Sikh guru and deity were honoured. Then extensive praise was given to the Hindu god Rama (seventh incarnation of Vishnu). He was repeatedly proclaimed as lord and king. In the whole service there was only one specific reference to Christ – namely a single trinitarian line in the final hymn.

On 12th March 1990 'An Observance for Commonwealth Day' was held in Westminster Abbey in the presence of the Queen. This was a clear example of inter-faith worship and of how the Commonwealth so easily leads us into such compromise. The 'observance' (which was indistinguishable from a service) included the reading of a 'Discourse of The Buddha' on how to attain Nirvana. There followed an exhortation from the Svetavatara Upanishad to worship God. The God here is, of course, Brahma, the creator-god of Hinduism. After this came a reading in praise of Allah.

In the concluding prayers a Buddhist representative urged praise to Buddha:

> Praise, denizens of earth
> and skies, praise, beings all,
> the Buddha, dear to gods
> and men, – who brings the Truth;
> – and may a blessing come.

The Islamic representative prayed:

> All praise be to Allah, Lord of the Worlds.
> The Beneficent, the Merciful.
> Master of the Day of Judgment.
> Thee (alone) we worship: Thee (alone) we ask
>   for help.

This writer cannot recognise Allah as God and the exclusive last line should be seen in the context of the repeated Islamic rejections of the idea that God has a son.

The name of Jesus was only mentioned twice in the printed order of service: at the end of prayers by the Moderator of the Free Church Federal Council and the Moderator of the General Assembly of the Church of Scotland. There was no worship addressed specifically to Jesus by name.

On Sunday 23rd October 1988 'An Inter-Faith Service' to mark the beginning of One World Week was held in the Chapter House of Bristol Cathedral. In this the Baha'is affirmed 'the fundamental oneness of religion' (which contradicts the exclusivism of Christianity). The Buddhists affirmed 'the teaching of the Buddhas. Lead a righteous life, not one that is corrupt. The righteous will live happily, both in this world and the next.' (This contradicts the Gospel of salvation through Jesus Christ rather than good works.) Following a Buddhist chant the Hindus made their contribution ending with 'a chant or devotional song from ladies of the Hindu community'.

Later the Muslims read from the Koran, 'We believe in Allah, and the revelation given to us, and to Abraham, Ismail, Isaac, Jacob and the tribes, and that given to Moses and Jesus and that given to (all) Prophets from our Lord; We make no difference between one and another of them.' (So they, typically, relegate Jesus to the level of a mere prophet.)

In the written liturgy the Christian contribution contained no reference to the name of Jesus Christ. Ironically, his name was briefly mentioned only in the Bahai and Muslim contributions.

On 15th September 1989 there was a multi-faith service in Canterbury Cathedral. This was not the Sunday eucharist led by the Archbishop of Canterbury but a short service on a Friday. Multi-faith pilgrimages (one led by a Bahai, another by a Buddhist) converged on the cathedral to worship and pray together. Although the liturgy included some biblical material (mainly from Psalms and Proverbs) it contained no mention of the name of Jesus Christ. Not even the prayers were in his name. The wording was carefully compiled to facilitate inter-faith worship.

The writer peacefully distributed a Christian evangelistic leaflet which warned of the New Age dangers of this event. When he did so within the cathedral precincts the church authorities called the police to prevent his continuing. Yet people of other faiths were freely worshipping their deities on church property and offering recruitment literature (including material for children). Not only are church authorities determined to continue these inter-faith events, so compromising the Christian faith, they are clearly determined to do all in their power to stop opposition to this trend. Apparently unaware of the New Age movement and its dangers, they are nevertheless furthering its aim to infiltrate the Church, bringing in the influence of oriental religion and occultism.

The New Age Christ

The New Age movement tends to put greater stress on the return of Christ than do many Christians. On the face of it this seems to be a mark of orthodoxy. Take, for example, the writings of a very prominent leader in the New Age movement – Alice Bailey. (She claims to have received their content by telepathy from the Tibetan Master Djwhal Khul.) She regularly refers to the return of Christ, quoting him from the New Testament about not being afraid of those who can merely kill the body; not judging; and about life more abundant. She also talks of the fellowship of Christ's sufferings and of his humble submission in the Garden of Gethsemane.[36]

She refers with approval to the life of the indwelling Christ.[37] When Christ comes he will 'see of the travail of his soul and be satisfied'.[38] All of this seems orthodox until one begins to search more carefully into Alice Bailey's prolific writings. We discover that Christ's coming must be prepared for by evil being routed.[39] 'The major point to be emphasised in the preparatory work for the return of Christ, is the establishing of right human relations. This has already been started by men of goodwill all over the world, under their many names.'[40]

In fact, says Bailey, there is a specific group of people preparing for Christ's return:

> The general staff of the Christ is already active in the form of the N.G.W.S. [New Group of World Servers]; they are as potent a body of forerunners as has ever preceded a great world Figure into the arena of mankind's living. Their work and influence is already seen and felt in every land, and nothing can destroy that which they have accomplished.[41]

But we find that these servers are from every religion and that 'their work will be largely to summarise and make effective the work of the two Sons of God: the Buddha and the Christ'.[42]

Here we begin to see clearly that Alice Bailey's teaching is contrary to that of Scripture. She continues: 'The Christ stands in patient silence, attentive to the effort that will make his work materialize on earth, and enable him to consummate the effort he made 2,000 years ago in Palestine. The Buddha hovers over the planet, ready to play His part if the opportunity is offered to him by mankind.'[43] In fact, she says, 'the appearance of the Great Lord . . . will date from a certain Wesak festival . . . Hence the gradual recognition of the Wesak festival, and its true significance in the occident is desirable . . .'[44] (see earlier on St James's, Piccadilly).

Bailey is against the exclusivism of Christianity: 'The day is dawning when all religions will be regarded as emanating from one great spiritual source; all will be seen as unitedly providing the one root out of which the universal world religion will inevitably emerge.'[45]

In view of all this we may well ask who the Christ is, in Alice Bailey's opinion. Apparently, he is the head of a hierarchy of Spiritual Masters.[46] He is the healer and the saviour who once worked through the apostles but now through New Age groups who follow both Buddha and the Christ.[47]

The spiritual hierarchy under the Christ will appear and take physical control of world affairs:

> Judaism will be fast disappearing; Buddhism will be spreading and becoming increasingly dogmatic; Christianity will be in a state of chaotic divisions and upheavals. When this takes place and the situation is acute enough the Master Jesus will take certain initial steps towards reassuming control of His Church; the Buddha will send two trained disciples to reform Buddhism; other steps will also be taken in this department of religion and education, over which the Christ rules . . .[48]

Now it is clear that this Christ is not the same as Jesus. Jesus is merely a Master – not the Christ. In fact, 'the Christ used the body of the initiate Jesus, taking possession of it at the time of the Baptism'.[49]

Bailey wants there to be 'a recognition of the claims of Christ (no matter by what name He may be called in the East or in the West)'.[50] In other words this is an inter-faith Christ – not Jesus Christ. According to her this Christ will not come 'as a conquering hero as the theological teachers have led man to believe'. Nor will he be the Messiah of the Jews:

> He will not come to convert the 'heathen' world, for in the eyes of the Christ and of His true disciples, no such world exists and

the so-called heathen have demonstrated historically less of the evil of vicious conflict than has the militant Christian world . . . The major effect of His appearance will surely be to demonstrate in every land the effects of *a spirit of inclusiveness* – an inclusiveness which will be channelled or expressed through Him. All who seek right human relations will be gathered automatically to Him, whether they are in one of the great world religions or not: all who see no true or basic difference between religion and religion, or between man and man, or nation and nation, will rally round Him; Those who embody the spirit of exclusiveness and separativeness will stand automatically and equally revealed and all men will know them for what they are.[51]

This Christ is none other than the Antichrist whom the New Testament says denies that Jesus is the divine Christ,[52] and who is no mere political or military leader but claims to be above all gods and even claims to be God. He will be able to manifest all kinds of counterfeit miracles, signs and wonders. Many people will believe his lies, that he is God.[53] (For details of recent reaffirmations of Alice Bailey's predictions of the Christ, see the writer's book *Our God Reigns*.)[54]

The New Age movement is a man-centred religion seeking 'religious experience' largely for its own sake through manipulation of the human mind, by oriental religions and occult techniques. It is infiltrating the Church, mainly as a result of and partly as a reaction to liberal theology. At the centre of the movement is a very strong syncretistic tendency seeking to amalgamate the various religions. This tendency will be a preparation for and will be completed by the return of the New Age, inter-faith Christ. This Christ is not Jesus Christ but what the New Testament describes as the Antichrist.

5

Reincarnation

Reincarnation in Western Culture

On the 7th December 1977 Eldon McCorkhill, 33, and Linda Cummings, 28, were sitting in a bar in Redlands, California, having a few drinks and chatting. The subject eventually turned to life after death, and Linda told Eldon that she was firmly convinced of the reality of re-incarnation. Eldon, with all his arrogant Western cultural mind-set behind him, scoffed loudly and a lively debate ensued. Voices were raised; conversation developed into debate; debate developed into argument. They argued all the way back to McCorkhill's apartment. Once they got there, he pulled a loaded pistol out of his drawer and handed it to her. 'If you believe in this,' he said, 'let's see what you'll come back as.' Linda took the gun, pointed it to her head and pulled the trigger.[1]

While this true story is hardly an accurate reflection of the influence of belief in reincarnation in the United States of America today, it does underscore an undeniable fact: belief in reincarnation has been growing rapidly in the Western world. Nothing could be further from the truth than that reincarnation is regarded in the West as fringe lunacy or oriental occult superstition. It may have been so regarded at the beginning of the twentieth century, but not today towards its end. Reincarnation is no fad. Stories of hypnotic 'regressions' and spontaneous 'recalls of former lives' are reasonably regular features in newspapers and magazines.

Most of us have had experiences of déjà vu: you feel that

you have been in this place before; had this conversation before; confronted these circumstances before; wrestled with this problem before; felt this disgust or exhilaration before; although consciously you know that it is not the case. In French, déjà vu literally means 'already seen'. Webster's dictionary describes it as being, 'In psychology, the illusion that one has previously had a given experience.' This experience has been capitalised in the reincarnation scene, with testimonies of previous existences secured under hypnosis being used to explain the whole déjà vu phenomenon.

A multitude of gurus, gopis, lamas, psychics and living masters have surfaced in this century in Europe as well as in the United States and have offered an almost endless variety of speculative metaphysical philosophies, many of which find their ideological foundations in the traditional religions of the East. One of the basic tenets of these religions is the ancient doctrine of reincarnation or rebirth (also called 'transmigration' or 'metapsychosis'): the idea that our soul or essence is in some way passed on after we die and injected into a new body at birth. This has been an essential element of Hindu and Buddhist thought since well before the birth of Christ and it still constitutes one of the central presuppositions of the Eastern world view of life in general and religion in particular. It is estimated that one third to one half of the world's population adhere to this concept.

In 1969, a Gallup Poll in the West indicated that an average of twenty to twenty-five per cent (depending on the country) of the population of Western Europe and North America either believed in reincarnation or at least considered it to be a good possibility (the breakdown: Austria 20 per cent; Canada 26 per cent; France 23 per cent; Britain 18 per cent; Sweden 12 per cent; USA 20 per cent; West Germany 25 per cent). No doubt these figures have increased rather than decreased as we move towards the twenty-first century.

Have we led past lives? Are we destined to return to this

earth again? Can we, under the right circumstances, recall former lives? Adherents to the New Age movement, like Shirley MacLaine, say 'yes' to these questions and recount fascinating tales of their former lives.

'Say a prayer to your higher self and Almighty God. Your mental body will leave your physical body and come back down in this life having the answers to the questions you have posed.' This counsel was given to a patient by a psychiatrist who practises 'past-lives therapy'. His patient wanted to know why she was blind in one eye. Under a hypnotic state she supposedly regressed in time and saw herself in New York. Her mental journey had taken her back to 1943 when she found herself in the body of another person hurling a bottle at her lover's face. As the psychiatrist moved her forward in time, she once again saw her boyfriend, this time with a patch over his eye. Now she was ready to return to her body. The answer was plain. She had committed a sin of violence in her last reincarnation, and in this life she had to be punished in order to work out her 'Karma'. What lesson had she learned? 'My higher self says I must learn to control myself in this life,' she replied to the psychiatrist.[2]

This story is true. Whether the facts are accurate is certainly open to question. The only certainty is that practitioners of 'past-lives therapy' have busy appointment schedules. It seems that in our stressful and tense culture there is a great reluctance to assume personal responsibility for the consequences of our conduct. It is much easier to blame everything on a former existence. Hindus, of course, have been doing this for centuries. New Age is no new religion but only a very old religion dressed in more modern (and Western) clothes. Many Westerners are following the same Karmic path of fatalism. The classic question of, 'Who am I?' is being replaced by the even more puzzling question, 'Who was I?'

The shift away from Church directives (even in the most authoritative Church structures) and moral absolutes has created a desperate need within our society to explain the nature of its existence. Man is incurably religious and the disintegration of faith within our Judaeo-Christian culture has not resulted in atheism. Man will normally seek to satisfy the spiritual vacuum created by the denial of God as a guiding force in his life. The occult explosion which has occurred this century only illustrates that Western man has traded his unbelief for a new system of order and meaning. Astrology, psychic predictions, and parapsychological investigations have all become pillars of his new 'religious' system, with reincarnation as a very significant part of its foundation.

So it is that reincarnation has become respectable within our culture. A variety of cults consider reincarnation to be an essential part of their teachings. Scientology, for example, proposes to remove the traumas of past lives by use of a device called an E-meter. Almost all the important Eastern cults base their quest for higher consciousness on the premise of reincarnation. Other groups embracing this belief include Rosicrucianism, the Unity School of Christianity, Hare Krishna, theosophy and Urantia. Reincarnation, however, is not confined to exotic cults. Many ordinary people believe that human events experienced in the past are passed on to affect the lives of people in the future.

What is Reincarnation?

The word 'reincarnation' comes basically from two Latin words 'in' and 'carnis' which taken together mean 'in the flesh'. When the prefix 're' is added it can easily be seen that reincarnation fundamentally means 'in the flesh again'. Reincarnation then, in essence, refers to the cyclical evolution of each man's soul as it passes into another body after death. The process continues until the soul has been chiselled and moulded to a state of perfection when it is able with little difficulty to merge back with its source.

In the pure theory of reincarnation, the soul can only inhabit another *human* body. The jest: 'Don't kick the cat; it may be your grandmother,' would not be regarded as tenable. On the other hand, transmigration, the Hindu doctrine from which reincarnation originated, asserts that each successive cycle may result in the soul incorporating itself in organic or inorganic life, meaning anything from a bird to a stone. The choice really depends upon the Karma accumulated by the soul in its previous reincarnations. Western advocates of 'rebirthing' have generally emphasised reincarnation rather than transmigration, however, knowing that the principles of the latter might be rejected by the more educated potential devotee. The average Westerner would not be so easily offended by the possibility of reincarnating as a respectable and rational human being, but the thought of coming back as a seagull or a spider would not be so enticing.

Unexpectedly, the doctrine of Karma has found acceptance among those from the West. In the earliest Hindu writings Karma was an act of ritual significance. Much later on, however, it was modified to illustrate how events in this life affect the quality of life in the next incarnation. Eventually Karma came to represent the immutable law of sowing and reaping, with pronounced punishment in future lives as a purification from evil in this life. Karma is 'an inexorable law of retributive justice . . . an internal law of nature independent of . . . the gods'.[3] Unlike the biblical law of sowing and reaping (Galatians 6:7) Karma has no final judgment. Its consequences are felt in this life, and the next, and thence on and on. Every response, reaction and act in this life influences the fate of the immortal soul's next incarnation. The healthy and the wealthy are seen to have accumulated good Karma in a previous life, while the less fortunate are seen to be getting their just reward for past sins. In other words, sin and punishment are precisely adjusted on a divine scale. So intensely is this believed that some Hindus or Buddhists would hesitate to help someone who was drowning or rescue someone caught in a fire, lest they interfere with Karma; perhaps that person deliberately drowned someone in the last life or intentionally left someone to burn in a blazing house. Fear of Karmic retribution often becomes extreme and causes a cold and fatalistic attitude. This inevitably generates a callous lack of concern for the needs of others, or can cause great confusion for a person when facing simple moral choices. To help or not to help – how will my decision and what I do as a result affect me?

Karma and justice appear to dovetail so perfectly that they are an almost irresistible pair. Do you know an impossible, arrogant, obnoxious person who always gets his own way? Or do you know someone who is loving, kind, generous and compassionate for whom everything goes wrong? This is a phenomenon in life which puzzles and troubles many and is partly the reason why Karma and reincarnation itself have a strong appeal to so many fair-minded people. How right it seems that the bad should somehow and at sometimes get their just desserts; and by the same token the good should get their just reward.

All of this is fair-sounding, but it has general fatal flaws and raises many searching questions. For example, if Karma really exists why is it that human nature has not been changed by it by now? History tells us what we have been; the daily newspapers tell us what we are. It is a simple verifiable fact that the twentieth century has been called the Century of Blood. As we have already noted, there have been more wars in this century than in any other: millions have died or been brutally maimed as a result of man's greed, fear, suspicion, vulnerability and pride. If history is to be our gauge then man has never changed: some would even say he has declined.

Again, if an individual is ignorant of prior experiences, how can he possibly learn from them? It is difficult enough to learn from things which are clearly and plainly taught – but to be unaware poses an enormous question. Yet again: if knowledge of our former lives would help us, would it not be in the nature of God to make that information available to us all? In any case, who supervises all this Karmic interaction to get results? There seems to be an uneasy silence to such questions.

Is it simply that we are looking for excuses for our behaviour? Or does believing that you had a terrible temper in another life exonerate you from responsibility to control it now?

Reincarnation supposes a mystical reason for birth defects – however these may show themselves. Prenatal care and medical supervision has done a great deal to reduce their number. Does 'Karmic law' then make prenatal care immoral?

If the poor and suffering deserve their plight, does the addition of a hospital; or the sinking of a well; or the rotation of the crops; or the compassion of a Mother Teresa, help or ultimately make things worse? Is it possible to call such care and compassion evil?

Since India has supposedly been the hub of 'spiritual awareness' for thousands of years due to reincarnation and Karmic teachings, why is the misery there among the world's worst?

If any society erases standards – or even blurs them – for judging good and evil can we not immediately see that anarchy and private chaos must result?

What is fair about a 'Karmic Law' which gives no rules and leaves one constantly guessing? How and why is the world's population increasing if there are no 'new' souls being added? If 'old' souls are being absorbed back into 'being' and all souls are immortal (having no end or beginning) how could there be enough souls to go around?

Are the rich and the healthy really better people than the poor and sick?

Christian Forgiveness Versus Reincarnation

The doctrine of Karma not only baffles the mind but contradicts the declarations of the Bible. In the system of

Karma, there is no forgiving Saviour to redeem one from the consequences of one's deeds. The action of Karma keeps moving onward, adding good or evil to its credit in a merciless manner. Though all Hindus seek 'Moksha', that is, liberation from the bondage of Karma, most resign themselves to the fact that they may need to be reborn millions of times to accomplish the feat. The glory of the Gospel of Christ is that, although each person is accountable to God, he or she can also become a new, forgiven creation in this life (2 Corinthians 5:17). Perhaps the most direct biblical account refuting Karma is to be found in that moving incident in the Gospel where Jesus encounters a man who had been born blind (John 9:1–3 GNB). Jesus's disciples asked him, 'Teacher, whose sin caused him to be born blind? Was it his own or his parents' sin?' In other words, 'Does his present affliction come to him because of a past life?' Jesus answers their query simply and directly: 'His blindness has nothing to do with his sins or his parents' sins.'

Some years ago I went with my family to the borders of Scotland. The house we had rented had a fine library. I enjoyed scanning the books there and picked a number which I read during the holiday. One of these was Lord Longford's autobiography in which he devotes quite a lot of space to his contact and correspondence with Ian Brady and Myra Hindley – the Moors murderers now in prison for arguably the most horrific series of murders on children this century. As the details of their crimes became known, the whole nation was appalled and stunned. Lord Longford tells how Myra Hindley was baptised a Catholic but was not brought up as one. She wrote from prison on one occasion to him, 'I wish I could put complete trust in God, but I am frightened to do so, for my faith is full of doubt and despair that I'll never be good enough to merit complete forgiveness . . .' Not so very much later she wrote again to Lord Longford:

I don't think that I could adequately explain just how much it means to me to have been to Confession and received Holy Communion. It is a terrifyingly beautiful thing; terrifying because I have taken a step which has taken me on to the threshold of a completely new way of life, which demands so much more from me than my previous one, and beautiful because I feel spiritually reborn. I made such a mess of my old life and I thank God for this second chance . . . it doesn't matter whether I live in prison or outside.[4]

In spite of the awesomeness of the crime – and no one would deny that – there is a completeness about the forgiveness which God gives and the freedom which that brings from all that is past. For the Christian the past has to be recognised and repented of. From that moment onwards the miracle of reconciliation with God and redemption from sin's guilt and power takes place. So it is that in the eighteenth century Charles Wesley wrote amidst his other 6,000 songs:

> For you and for me
> He prayed on the tree:
> The prayer is accepted, the sinner is free.
> The sinner am I,
> Who on Jesus rely,
> And come for the pardon God cannot deny.
> His death is my plea:
> My advocate see,
> And hear the blood speak that hath answered for me;
> He purchased the grace
> Which now I embrace:
> O Father, Thou knowest He hath died in my place![5]

Karma is unnecessary in the light of the cross of Jesus Christ.

What Really Happens to the Body and Soul After Death?

The doctrine of reincarnation which influences so many New Age cults is an integral and foundational belief of

Hinduism. The Hindu views his physical nature as the source of his soul's bondage. Even animals are subject to the cycles of rebirth known as 'Samsara'. Christianity too, since Jesus Christ – the man who was God – came in human flesh, lays a great emphasis on the human body. However, biblically and in every major Christian creed, there is a simple statement about the resurrection of the body. One day the same kind of body in which Jesus rose from the grave and in which he spent six weeks with his disciples – talking to them, giving them Bible studies, eating with them, and generally sharing their lives, and in which he ascended to the right hand of God – will be ours. Before his death Jesus emphasised his spiritual reality. ('I am the Way, the truth, and the life' (John 14:6, GNB); 'I am the bread of life' (John 6:48, GNB); I am the resurrection and the life' (John 11:25, GNB)). After his resurrection he clearly emphasised his physical reality. He went to considerable lengths to point out that he was substantial; he wasn't a ghost ('Touch me and see; a ghost does not have flesh and bones' (Luke 24:39, NIV). He ate some of their breakfast which actually he had cooked – and there is something very substantial about that!) So today there is a man in heaven and his name is Jesus. We too one day will have a new body like his glorious body to enable us to explore the new heavens and the new earth. The Bible teaches that each human being will maintain his personal identity throughout eternity.

Some years ago the late Dr Harry Rimmer, an old American New Testament commentator, wrote a letter to a well-known Christian broadcaster in the United States called Charles E. Fuller. Harry Rimmer wrote:

Next Sunday you are to talk of heaven. I am interested in that land because I have held a clear title to a bit of property there for about fifty years. I did not buy it. It was given to me without price. But the donor purchased it for me at a tremendous sacrifice. I am not holding it for speculation. It is not a vacant lot. For more than half a century I have been sending materials up to the greatest Architect of the universe who has been building a home for me which will never need remodelling or repairing because it will suit me perfectly, individually, and will never grow old. Termites can never undermine its foundations, for it rests upon the 'Rock of Ages'. Fire cannot destroy it, floods cannot wash it away. No lock or bolts will ever be placed upon the doors. For no vicious person can ever enter the land where my dwelling stands, almost completed and almost ready for me to enter in and abide in peace eternally without fear of being ejected.

There is a valley of deep shadow between this place where I live and that to which I shall journey in a very short time. I cannot reach my home in that city without passing through this valley. But I am not afraid because the best Friend I ever had went through the same valley long, long ago and drove away all its gloom. He has stuck with me through thick and thin since we first became acquainted fifty-five years ago. And I own His promise in printed form never to forsake me or leave me alone. He will be with me as I walk through the valley of the shadow, and I shall not lose my way when He is with me. I hope to hear your sermon on heaven next Sunday, but I have no assurance that I will be able to do so. My ticket to heaven has no date marked for the journey, no return coupon, and no permit for baggage. Yes, I am ready to go, and I may not be here while you are talking next Sunday evening, but I will meet you there some day.

Harry Rimmer[6]

Harry Rimmer actually did die before the following Sunday.

What is this? Sentimentalism? Wishful thinking? Fantasy? No, it is truth based on the reality of the life, death, resurrection and ascension of Jesus Christ, and his words and assurances that death is not the end – only the end of the beginning.

This is so distinctively different from the Hindu who has concluded that the consciousness of the individual is irrelevant since he might come back after death as a monkey or a goat or even a plant or a rock (in more extreme Hinduistic thinking).

In spite of attempts to cite biblical evidence to support

reincarnation (for example, the Transfiguration of Jesus in the presence of three of his disciples in Matthew 17 and Jesus's bold statement in John 8:58 (GNB): 'Before Abraham was born, "I am"'), the Bible clearly indicates that, 'Everyone must die once' (Hebrews 9:27, GNB). In contrast to reincarnation's uncertain game of chance with life, Jesus indicated two destinations only for living souls: 'the resurrection of life', and 'the resurrection of judgment'. The basis for the theory of reincarnation is that man can eventually work out his own salvation, contrary to the Christian doctrine of grace. Grace is, of course, the heartland of the Christian Gospel: God loves us because he loves us and anything and all we receive from him is completely free and entirely undeserved. It is on the basis of the grace of God – the sheer undeserved generosity of his heart – that we have hope.

In addition, reincarnational doctrine marks a fundamental difference with Christianity in its view of creation. Hinduism sees each soul as but a portion of the First Cause with only legendary explanations as to how each being came into its original state of existence. This is in sharp contrast with the Genesis account of man's origin as occurring from a divine act of creation by a purposeful God possessing a moral will.

Since the doctrines of Karma and reincarnation leave man in despair with no hope, at the mercy of and victimised by the whole range of forces of cosmic chance, the Hindu thinkers needed to find some ray of hope to penetrate this darkness. Historically, the impact of Christianity forced Hinduism to come up with some method of illustrating the personality of an impersonal god, and so show the way to avoiding endless transmigrations. The theistic branch of Hinduism made the Unknowable God more approachable by suggesting that he would occasionally incarnate in some illusory form visible to man. Such a god-man is called an avatar. This event is not a constant occurrence, but only takes place once for each age when man is in desperate need of such assistance.

In all of this – reincarnation, Hinduism and New Age – there is a great emphasis on man and his need rather than upon God and his glory. There is also an awareness that what is being provided is the result of human thinking rather than the recording of clinical historical facts. One of the things which has always commended Christianity and baffled its critics has been the historical foundation of the Christian faith. In event after event there has always been encouragement to verify the facts empirically in the flesh-and-blood reality of history.

The Well Known Face of New Age: Shirley MacLaine

All movements have their well-known faces – those who espouse and 'front' the movement. New Age is no exception. As we have seen, one of its best known devotees is the beautiful, talented, famous, charming, intelligent and compassionate Shirley MacLaine. Her reincarnationist views are outspokenly declared in books, lectures and on televison. She speaks not only of her conclusions in thinking but also shares experiences, conversations and insights which have led her to her conclusions. Not only has she aligned herself with New Age thought, but she has gone far beyond reincarnation and Karma and into other occult fields. Many of Shirley MacLaine's beliefs have been dealt with elsewhere in this book. Her concept of 'trans-channelling' is merely a new name for mediumship. The Bible, of course, never denies the reality of the spirit-world – indeed it confirms its reality. Nor does the Bible deny the possibility of human contact with the spirit world while here on earth. In fact, the Bible is concerned that we should not be deceived and urges us to 'test the spirits' (1 John 4:1, NIV). We are encouraged to pray to the Father, through the Son by means of the enabling Holy Spirit and at the same time to flee from Satan and his deceptions. It is unbelievably dangerous to get 'caught' in the spirit world of the dominion of darkness. Whatever is labelled 'spiritual'

or experienced 'spiritually' has to be tested to ensure
whether it is of God or the devil.

For example, Shirley MacLaine speaks of 'Astral' guides
who lead her. Jesus, however, on that momentous final
briefing he gave his disciples on the eve of his crucifixion,
says categorically that it is the Spirit of Truth (the Holy
Spirit) who will guide us into all the truth (John 16:13
GNB). There are evil spirits but they are not truthful. Their
stock-in-trade is to deceive us, and they will do so by their
plausibility, their knowledge, their authority, and often
their kindness. In the experience of such demonic manifestation it is important to insist on an answer to the
question: 'Did Jesus Christ, the Son of God, come to earth
as a human being and has He been truly raised from the
dead?' It would be interesting in such a spirit-dialogue (not
that it is to be sought or commended!) to ask why no spirit
ever describes a former life of a born-again Christian, filled
with the Holy Spirit of God.

Shirley MacLaine clearly believes that nothing happens
by accident, and that every little thing serves a purpose of
some kind, however obscure. However, this fatalistic view
of life is hard to support in the light of the facts. We live in a
natural world where accidents can and do happen. God
respects the laws of nature which he devised and will
generally interfere with them only as a result of the direct
and specific prayer requests of his family on earth. Most of
the 'bad things' which occur are caused directly or indirectly by the selfishness, carelessness, indifference or sinfulness
of people. As we come to know God as he is revealed to us
in the Bible, and particularly in his Son Jesus Christ, we
discover his character and conclude that many of those 'bad
things' are not according to his perfect will. The experience
of many Christians is that tragedy does strike them.
However, God has affirmed that he will never leave us to
face those situations alone; he will walk with us through
them and in His own sovereign way turn them to good for us
as we trust him and depend on him.

Shirley MacLaine is only one among many others – some

consciously but many unconsciously – who are leading us away from biblical truth. As the generations become more and more spiritually and biblically illiterate it is inevitable that error will become indistinguishable from truth and will therefore be dismissed. Since many do not recognise Hinduism or witchcraft or the like, what is written, seen or done passes unnoticed into the thinking and educating of a new generation – and few protest.

The Mutually Exclusive: Reincarnation and Christian Doctrine

For Christians who consider the matter it will quickly become clear that reincarnation and the Scriptures are mutually exclusive. The reincarnationist's response to the problem of human sin, wrong-doing and failure, with its countless opportunities of reformation, cannot stand alongside the complete and perfect work of the redemption of Jesus Christ. This central feature of biblical revelation and Christian conviction of the sacrifice of Christ on the cross and the shedding of his blood for the sins of the world can never be compatible with a system of belief which denies his atonement. In addition, the law and function of Karma inhibits any choice of the will to determine a life of obedience to God's plans. It is a selfish concept that sees no merit in sacrifice for the welfare of others, and only despair and resignation, not hope, are its result. Reincarnation offers no loving God, no forgiving grace, and dismisses any concept of an Almighty God whose nature is to have mercy.

The apostle Paul writing to the young Christian leader, Timothy, urges him to have nothing to do with any belief or practice which comes of demonic inspiration (1 Timothy 4:1–7). This must certainly be so in the case of reincarnation for it seeks to replace the hope of the Christian faith – the resurrection. Without doubt the greatest chapter on the resurrection in the New Testament is the fifteenth chapter of First Corinthians. There it simply says: 'And if Christ has not been raised, then your faith is a delusion and you are still lost in your sins' (15:17, GNB). It is hardly to be wondered at that a thick fatalistic gloom permeates any religious system which upholds reincarnation. So it is in that same chapter of that same letter to the Christians in Corinth that Paul says: 'If our hope in Christ is good for this life only and no more, then we deserve more pity than anyone else in all the world' (15:19, GNB). It is the promise of eternal life with Jesus – begun here and now – but transformed beyond the grave into a glorious reality that brings worth and meaning to serving Christ in this life.

In that remarkable Old Testament book – Daniel – the reader is reminded that, 'Many of those who have already died will live again: some will enjoy eternal life, and some will suffer eternal disgrace' (Daniel: 12:3, GNB). Such is the early foreshadowing of the hope of Christ's victory over death. Jesus affirmed the same alternatives in the fourth Gospel: 'Whoever believes in the Son has eternal life; whoever disobeys the Son will not have life, but will remain under God's punishment' (John 3:36, GNB). Jesus, of course, offered the proof of his own body to substantiate his promise. Before his death he emphasised his spiritual characteristics, but after his resurrection he emphasised his physical characteristics. So it was that he invited the doubter, Thomas, to put his hand in his side, and challenged his disciples to touch him so that they could be sure that he was not a ghost but flesh and bones. Over a period of forty days over 500 of his followers – both in public and in private, corporately as well as individually – witnessed this infallible proof, and so doubt that the dark horror of death was final was swept away.

Instead of giving instructions to prepare for successive reincarnations, Jesus gave directions to prepare for the day when they too would be raised from the dead to be with him for ever! 'Those who have died believing in Christ will rise to life first,' cries Paul, 'then we who are living at that time will be gathered up along with them in the clouds to meet the Lord in the air. And so we will always be with the Lord.' He continues by saying: 'So then, encourage one another with these words' (1 Thessalonians 4:16–18, GNB).

6

The Environment as Religion

Quite a lot of you have written to me during the last year or so, saying how worried you are about the future of our planet. Many of you will have heard of the greenhouse effect, and perhaps you've heard, too, about even more urgent problems caused by the pollution of our rivers and seas and the cutting down of the great forests . . . the future of all life on Earth depends on how we behave towards one another, and how we treat the plants and animals that share our world with us.

So said the Queen in her Christmas message in 1989. The whole thrust of her speech was on conservation.

Prince Philip, in his 1988 Presidential Address to the Royal Society, predicted the demise of the human race through pollution of the environment. The Royal Family are in tune with the new emphasis on ecology which has developed in the 1980s.

The Green Revolution

Jonathon Porritt, Director of Friends of the Earth, admitted on television recently that he was amazed at the speed of the Green Revolution during the 1980s.[1] Various events during the eighties have contributed to this revolution. The Bhopal disaster in 1984 when over 2,000 people were killed by cyanide gas was one. Then in 1985 the British Antarctic Survey discovered a huge 'hole' in the ozone layer which protects us from the harmful effects of the sun's ultraviolet rays. Two years later it was established that this had been caused by chlorofluorocarbons (CFCs) used in refrigerators and aerosols.

In 1986 the explosion at the Chernobyl nuclear power station in the USSR showed the horrific possibilities of nuclear destruction of the environment. By 1988 the reality of the threat posed by the greenhouse effect had become widely acknowledged. It was seen that the warming of the atmosphere through carbon dioxide produced by motor vehicles and coal-fired power stations could lead to crop failure, tempestuous weather and disastrous rises in sea levels.

On 27th September 1988 Margaret Thatcher gave her famous 'Green speech' to the Royal Society. She said: 'Protecting the balance of nature is one of the great challenges of the late twentieth century.'[2] This was the first speech by a world leader on this subject and had widespread effect. Even Margaret Thatcher, protagonist of free enterprise, had gone green. Such was the strength of the Green Revolution.

One aspect of this phenomenon has been the emergence of the Green Party which showed remarkable popularity in the recent European elections. Their election material uses apocalyptic language concerning impending ecological disaster:

> Every day there are new horror stories in the papers and on T.V. about the end of the world. And it's not science fiction. It's a here-and-now fact. We're killing our own planet with our crazy way of life: polluting the air we breathe, the water we drink and the earth that grows our food . . . Without your vote, the chances of our planet surviving into the 21st century will be slim.

They refer to the effects of chemicals in food, hormones fed to animals and impure water. Then,

> Our coasts are strewn with stinking sewage, oil and toxic waste. The seals and dolphins are dying, and some fish are too

contaminated to eat . . . the Greenhouse Effect . . . won't mean more sunny days, but floods, storms and damage. London, East Anglia and many other coastal areas would end up under water. The soil could blow away leaving deserts where crops used to grow – unless we act now.[3]

They also point out that,

while governments talk about global warming caused by carbon dioxide pollution, the forest lungs of the world are being destroyed. [Trees absorb carbon dioxide and emit oxygen.] Of the 16 million square kilometres of tropical rainforest standing a century ago, only 9 million are left. Not only are we losing valuable resources and habitats; entire tribes are losing their ancestral homes. In last autumn's 'burning season' alone, more than 4% of the Amazon rainforest – an area the size of the United Kingdom – was lost.[4]

It would be quite wrong to deny that we are facing serious ecological problems. But it is worth noting that the apocalyptic language which has done so much to bring about the Green Revolution is not necessarily verifiable. For example, whilst some Greens maintain that global temperature has increased by 0.5° C since the mid 1980s, Dr John Houghton, head of the Meteorological Office, said there has been an increase of 0.5° C in the last century.[5] The environmental group Ark estimate that if the polar ice cap begins to melt, the sea level will rise by 1.5 metres in the year 2030 and possibly by over eighteen feet by 2050. So most of central London would be under water. But Dr Peter Wadhams, Director of the Scott Polar Research Institute, has dismissed this as 'irresponsible and harmful'.[6]

It is also very difficult to obtain detailed information about the tropical rain-forests. The United Nations published a report in 1982 estimating that between 1976 and 1980 moist tropical forests were being cleared at an annual rate of 0.6 per cent and 'virgin' forests by 0.27 per cent.[7] This makes the apocalyptic language of the Greens seem grossly exaggerated. One conservation group claims that

300,000 square kilometres of Amazonian rain-forest were cleared in September 1988 alone. But Dr Phil Fearnside of the Amazon Research Institute claims that only 35,000 square kilometres were cleared in the whole of 1988.[8] In 1980 environmentalist Norman Myers, working for the US National Research Council, concluded that 220,000 square kilometres of forest were cleared each year. That is an area equivalent to that of the UK. But the Council was concerned about his methods and commissioned a re-examination of his figures. As a result Myers reduced his estimates by two-thirds.[9] as we have seen, the Greens still quote the earlier figure.

I am reminded of a booklet published by the United Nations Centre for Economic and Social Information in 1969. It was called 'The Challenge of a Decade – Global Development or Global Breakdown'.[10] It contained predictions of the problems the world would face in 1980. Here are some of them written as if they were 1980 news reports: 'The destruction of all life in the seas could occur in the immediate future. Such a development would cause the death of mankind.'[11] 'Flights to large areas in Asia, the Middle East and Africa were indefinitely suspended today. An enraged public in America, Australia and Europe demanded protection against the risk of Cholera, yellow fever, plague and other contagious diseases. These have reached pandemic proportions in many of the poorer areas of the world.'[12]

The fact is that the alarmist and exaggerated warnings of the Greens are being taken up by the mass media. And they are largely responsible for the Green Revolution. But, as we shall see later, this revolution is also leading many people into New Age thinking and experience.

Biblical Ecology

The starting-point of biblical ecology is that the Christian faith is based on a personal relationship with God, who is the creator of the world. It is even more personal when we read that God made the universe through Christ and for him. And it is Christ who sustains all things by his powerful word.[13]

There is a perhaps rather sentimental nineteenth-century hymn ('Loved with everlasting love' by G. W. Robinson) which expresses this:

> Heaven above is softer blue,
> Earth around is sweeter green;
> Something lives in every hue
> Christless eyes have never seen;
> Birds with gladder songs o'erflow,
> Flowers with deeper beauty shine,
> Since I know, as now I know,
> I am his and he is mine.

But man is no mere part of creation. He is the high point of divine creativity, a special creation in the image and likeness of God. As such, he was given the authority to rule or to have dominion over nature.[14] But as with all human rule, delegated by God, it does not mean domination and exploitation.

The Bible clearly intends man to care for creation. He was set in the garden of Eden 'to work it and take care of it'.[15] We are stewards, not owners, of creation. Hence we should treat it with reverence as God's possession entrusted to our care.

For example, Old Testament law ordained that every seventh year was a sabbatical year when the land must be allowed to lie fallow and recover from the years of use, just as farm animals must be given a day off from work each week.[16] The land belongs to God not man. So every fiftieth year is the Year of Jubilee when land and property sold to Israelites revert to their original owners.[17]

Furthermore, God originally placed man in a beautiful parkland. 'Eden' means 'delight' or 'bliss'. This suggests that God intended us to appreciate the beauty of creation. Man is not made for ugly environments, yet many people in the world, not least in inner cities, are deprived of such beauty around them.

The dignity which God invested in creation is well illustrated in his Covenant made after the Flood. It was not just made with Noah and his descendants, but with 'every living creature', in fact, with 'all life on the earth'.[18]

Such is the importance of nature that God made a covenant with it. The Bible teaches that every time we see a rainbow we should remember that.

But things were spoilt through the Fall of Man, that is, the act of sinful disobedience to God in the Garden of Eden. Instead of enjoying fulfilling work tending a beautiful garden or park, man now had to be involved in 'painful toil' to work the garden which was cursed with thorns and thistles.[19]

So through sin, man's relationship with God, with his fellow humans and with nature was spoilt. Those who have received forgiveness through a faith commitment to Christ ought, therefore, to be exemplary in relating to nature. Christians ought to be conservationists.

But, in fact, Christians have neglected this area and have even misunderstood the biblical teaching. Jonathon Porritt writes: 'It is precisely the confusion between "dominion" and "domination" that has provided Christianity with a licence for participating, often with uncommon enthusiasm, in the wholesale exploitation of the earth, eliminating a sense of reverence for God's creation.'[20] It is true that much of this exploitation has been carried out by merely nominal Christians. However, committed Christians have also neglected biblical ecology.

The Bible is also positive about the future of creation. Paul tells us that the whole of creation is subjected to frustration because of the sin of man and is groaning as it waits for liberation from bondage to decay. This will happen when the ultimate experience of human redemption takes place: when Christ appears again.[21]

In the end creation is so important that the cosmic

catastrophe of the end times[22] will lead to the transformation of nature.[23] There will be a new heaven and a new
earth.[24] All of this biblical teaching shows that Christians
should be in the forefront of the Green Revolution. This is
primarily because it is God's world which he invests with
great dignity. And he calls us to care for it with reverence.

The environment is a religious issue. Biblical Christianity
is green.

New Age Ecology

1. The Voice of Moderation: Jonathon Porritt

Jonathon Porritt is aware of the importance of the spiritual
aspect of the Green Movement in changing human attitudes. He writes: 'so many people in the Green Movement
have now begun to pay more and more attention to the
spiritual dimension of what it is that makes us green.'[25] And
elsewhere:

> The spiritual dimension of the Green Movement consists re-
> latively simply of two essential components. Firstly, the en-
> deavour to promote ecological wisdom in *all* existing religions
> and spiritual traditions, by drawing out the teaching practices
> already inherent in those traditions. Secondly, the need to find
> ways of letting people reconnect with the Earth, especially
> people who are otherwise untouched by religion, and possibly
> even embarrassed by the use of the word 'spiritual' . . . To heal
> that alienation we must now seek to re-present the abundance
> and the diversity of the natural world as the primary revelation
> of the Divine to most men and women.[26]

He acknowledges that there is a spectrum in the Green
Movement from the political leftists to the mystical super-
naturalists. However, he says: 'most Greens in this country
would still insist that without some understanding of the
spiritual dimension, it will always be a rather lifeless,
insipid shade of green that we are dealing with'.[27]

Porritt is very critical of much Christian attitude to

ecology. He puts it bluntly: 'Christianity, by taking the divine out of all that is earthly and lodging it in some distant and comprehensively male God-head, has managed only to endorse and indeed accelerate the pattern of ecological destruction that we now see.'[28]

On the other hand he believes that, 'Only Buddhism can make any real claim to being permeated through and through with ecological awareness and guidance about "right livelihood".'[29]

A major change in outlook favoured by the Greens is from an anthropocentric (human-centred) view of the world to a biocentric (life-centred) view of the world. The former makes the world subservient to man and can lead to the exploitation of nature. As we have noted, some nominal Christians have taken this line but theirs is a misunderstanding of biblical teaching. On the other hand, some Greens hold that all species, including man, are of equal value. Porritt regards these extremists as 'a bit dotty'.[30]

'But,' he says:

'the recognition of value inherent in all living nature' is an important part of an emerging green spirituality. It stems from the deep ecological awareness that nature and the self are one. And, as Fritjof Capra has pointed out, 'this is also the very core of spiritual awareness'. Indeed, when the concept of the human spirit is understood as the mode of consciousness in which the individual feels connected to the cosmos as a whole it becomes clear that ecological awareness is spiritual in its deepest essence, and that the new ecological ethics is grounded in spirituality.[31]

Later Porritt speaks positively of the New Age movement:

Learning how to reconnect with ourselves and with the Earth, and then learning how to celebrate that reconnection, is a very personal thing. It can be very confusing. The New Age Movement, for instance, covers a multitude of networks, communities, individuals, tendencies and gurus which it is almost impossible to sort out. All one can incontrovertibly claim is that many thousands in the U.K. have found in New Age thinking and teaching a sense of hope and meaning that has eluded them elsewhere.[32]

John Stewart Collis, whom Porritt regards as one of the most important visionaries of the Green Movement, wrote in 1972:

> This is now regarded as a very irreligious age. But perhaps it only means that the mind is moving from one state to another. The next stage is not a belief in many gods. It is not a belief in one God. It is not a belief at all – not a conception in the intellect. It is an extension of the consciousness so that we may *feel* God, or, if you will, an experience of harmony, an intonation of the Divine which will link us again with animism, the experience of unity lost and the in-break of self-consciousness.[33]

We have seen that such thinking is fundamental to the New Age movement. Porritt also quotes Richard North, environment correspondent of *The Independent*, who makes the illuminating statement:

> An awful lot of us just need to worship something. But in order to be able to worship, you have to be able to find something outside of yourself – and better than yourself. God is a construct for that. So is nature. We are all falling in love with the environment as an extension to and in lieu of having fallen out of love with God. As it happens, it makes for a pretty deficient religion, but as an object of worship, nature takes some beating.[34]

Jonathon Porritt concludes:

> Many Greens believe that salvation lies in opening our spirit to the presence of the divine in the world, acknowledging joyfully a sense of wonder and humility before the miracle of creation, and *then* going out and taking action to put things right, inspired by that vision.[35]

So Jonathon Porritt, who clearly stands in a moderate position over Green spirituality, nevertheless stresses its importance. He sees the importance of working with all the faiths to further ecological concern and he commends the ecological awareness of Buddhism. He is also positive about the New Age movement and favours seeking the divine in nature and connecting with the cosmos, all of which points in a pantheistic direction. As a prominent and respected spokesman for the Greens in Britain he makes it abundantly clear that the conservation movement is essentially spiritual. He also speaks in favour of the Gaia Hypothesis.

2. *The Gaia Hypothesis*

Dr James Lovelock, a British chemist, popularised this in 1979. It is described succinctly by Peter Russell, author of *The Awakening Earth*. He points out that when the first astronauts saw the earth from space,

> the whole planet looked as if it might be some huge single living system. They were in a sense having a direct intimation of what has now become known as the Gaia Hypothesis – so called after the Greek Earth goddess. This theory suggests that the whole of the Earth's biosphere functions together as a single living system, maintaining the optimum conditions for its continued existence and evolution. The different species might be likened to the different organs in a body, each having its own function, and each supporting the functioning of the body as a whole. Thus we might think of the tropical rain-forests as something akin to the liver [filtering out the waste carbon dioxide], and the oceans and atmosphere perform, among other things, the function of a circulatory system. Of course the timescales are very different. Our days and nights might be likened to the heartbeat of the planet; and the seasons are most like her breaths.

But what is the function of humanity?

> One possibility is that humanity is becoming a global brain. When we consider the ways in which telecommunications are

linking up across the planet, we find that there are indeed many parallels with the way the brain in an unborn child develops. Moreover, if the pace of development of information technology is sustained it will only take a decade or two till our global telecommunications network equals the complexity of the human brain.[36]

Russell then proceeds to state that, alternatively, humanity might be a 'form of planetary cancer' because of our destructive ways. He says: 'the Gaia Hypothesis suggests that the planet looks after its own welfare; she has no particular brief to preserve humanity. If we threaten the well-being of Gaia, then perhaps the best thing she could do would be to get rid of us.' He goes on to suggest that this could be by nuclear war or a nerve gas accident or AIDS.[37]

Lovelock saw this theory in a purely scientific way. And some Christians may see it as describing the natural laws God has 'written into' nature. But many will see it in a revival of pantheism. Also the negative view of the value of humanity is anti-Christian.

One prominent New Ager who promotes the Gaia Hypothesis is Sir George Trevelyan who taught Prince Philip at Gordonstoun. He founded the Wrekin Trust in 1971. The Trust is a non-denominational organisation dedicated to teaching on the spiritual nature of humanity and the holistic view of the universe. Trevelyan says: 'We must learn to think wholeness, to realise the reality of the Earth mother and that our exploitation of the animal kingdom and the rest of nature is piling up for us an enormous karmic debt.' He continues that the present world view is,

that we stand over and above Nature that is totally independent of us. The planet is assumed to be a dead mineral, the thinking being that we are free to exploit it for our own use and profit. We've developed so much intellectually over the last century but we've failed lamentably in our stewardship of the planet. It's a very grave thing and it's coming to a head.[38]

The Wrekin Trust organises conferences on astrology, meditation, alchemy, psychic awareness and earth mysteries.

> Certain places, often enhanced by the architectural form of the structures upon them, have gained a considerable historical reputation for containing a special quality that can shift perception to a deeper awareness of reality and awaken the sacred within. Recent research likening the Earth to a living being with its subtle force fields, has discerned underlying energy patterns which are focused at specific locations within the landscape. Historical and archaeological evidence suggests that peoples of the past recognised and used this energy in their religious practices, erecting their monuments in accordance with underlying geomantic [divination] principles.[39]

The theory behind this is occult but it explains why New Agers are interested in using ancient cathedrals for conservation events, normally of an inter-faith nature. One Wrekin Trust conference included a visit to Chartres Cathedral to 'explain the esoteric significance of the cathedral and its alchemical, astrological and spiritual symbolism.'[40]

Another conference organised by the Trust was to 'explore the profound teachings of the American Indians which can help us to re-connect with the wisdom of mother Earth and re-establish a harmonious relationship both with ourselves and the planet.'[41]

This thinking is, of course, related to the Gaia Hypothesis. And, in fact, the Wrekin Trust held a conference on 'Gaia, Evolution and Consciousness' in April 1989. The speakers included Jim Lovelock; Dewasenta, 'a clan mother of the Iroquois Nation and one of the few traditional Indians selected by tribal chiefs to take their teachings into Western culture'; and Hugh Montefiore, former Bishop of Birmingham.[42]

Trevelyan was involved in the organisation of the 'Harmonic Convergence' which took place in August 1987. New Agers gathered at sacred sites all over the world from sunrise on 16th August to sunrise on 18th August. The main English site was Glastonbury which is held to be a centre of mystical earth energy.

The leaflet produced for the Glastonbury event called 'Harmonic Convergence' quoted the ancient American Indian prophecy which is also used by Greenpeace. 'When the Earth is sick and the animals have disappeared, there will come a tribe of people from all cultures who believe in deeds not words and who will restore the Earth to its former beauty. This tribe will be called Warriors of the Rainbow.'

The whole event was seen as an earth healing or cleansing activity when peace and universal love were invoked on the planet. Trevelyan wrote in the leaflet:

> Planet Earth is in a precarious state as she enters the time of change at the threshold of the Aquarian Age. But we human beings are integrally part of nature, that point where she becomes self conscious and can look out into ethereal space. God is in us and is the life in all things. Unconditional love is the Divine Gift and as it floods through us it will bring about the cleansing of separated particles of humanity to restore undivided oneness . . . The cleansing change in the planet is on us, but will manifest in more violent ways if the harmonic convergence is not rightly initiated . . . We humans, rightful stewards of the planet, have failed lamentably and culpably in our stewardship and are rapidly turning our beautiful Terra into a desert – for profit! Planet Earth, Gaia, has sent up her prayer to God and this will not go unheeded. So this day will initiate a process which like a chain reaction, could flood through the human layer.

However, what Trevelyan writes later shows the great spiritual dangers involved in this exercise. He states:

> Apparently empty space is thronged with angelic beings, all facets of the colourful and infinitely varied Oneness. Holistic vision implies seeing ourselves, each and all, as facets of this stupendous Whole. So we hold our Celebration at this holy and sacred centre of Avalon. The object is to attune ourselves and lift consciousness so that the light can flood into the darkened

Earth. Know that our friends out of the body will crowd around us, blending with our thinking. Spiritual light will drive out the beings of darkness . . . Prophecies have seen the possibility of celestial beings manifesting.

This is the language of spiritualism and indicates the grave spiritual dangers in which these doubtless altruistic New Age conservationists are. Spiritualism is strongly condemned in Scripture as very dangerous to spiritual and emotional health.[43]

3. The Findhorn Community

Paul Hawken, an American businessman and author, heard about the amazing claims made for Findhorn. The community is situated on the Moray Firth at a place where the soil is very poor and the weather quite bleak. But reports from it said that forty-pound cabbages, sixty-pound broccoli and eight-foot delphiniums had been grown. Hawken, whose business interests are in horticulture, was as cynical about these reports as some readers may be. So he visited Findhorn, taking a very sceptical approach to the place.

He was amazed by what he experienced there and wrote an account of it in *The Magic of Findhorn*. Findhorn, like Glastonbury, is said to be on a 'cosmic power point'. People from all over the world visit it. Recently, middle-ranking politicians from around the world accepted an invitation to meet there to learn from this world-famous New Age centre.

Findhorn was founded by Peter and Eileen Caddy. Peter had contact with spiritualism from an early age.[44] Another formative influence was David Spangler who again had occult experiences as a child and has mediumistic powers.[45]

The first important discovery at Findhorn was of the Devas. Deva is a Hindu word for a god or good spirit. But the community 'think of Devas as angelic beings', and it seems that they design the archetypal pattern for each species and channel down the required energies for its manifestation on earth. The nature spirits, on the other hand, may be regarded as the builders 'who build up the plant' from the energies channelled down by the Devas.[46] In 1963 Dorothy Maclean, one of the Findhorn leaders, received a message from the spirit world which said:

> You are to co-operate in the garden by thinking about the Nature Spirits, the higher Nature Spirits, the Spirits of different physical forms, such as the spirits of the clouds, of rain, of the separate vegetables. In the new world their realm will be quite open to humans – or, should I say, humans will be quite open to them.[47]

Dorothy began to receive hundreds of messages from the Devas of individual plants telling her how to care for each one. Over a period of time an overall message became clear:

> The Devic world emphasized that man has to do one thing in order to reverse the trend of events on the planet: he has to recognize within himself the Divinity and wholeness of which he is part. He must touch the core which perceives itself as a part of all things, all beings, and all aspects of creation. In that recognition and touching the distinction between the outer and the inner is erased and vanishes.[48]

In 1966 Robert Ogilvie Crombie (known as Roc) became involved with Findhorn. One day in March of that year Crombie claimed to have begun to see nature spirits and to converse with them. It would be possible to write him off as a lunatic or a con man. But having read the accounts I must say they have a ring of an actual experience of the spirit world, although I don't necessarily agree with the identification of the spirits. Certainly they were believed by the Findhorn Community and had a profound influence on its life and teaching.

Crombie records a conversation with Pan (the Greek god of pastures, flocks and woods). Pan asks:

'Do you love me?'

'Yes!'

He looked at me with a strange smile and a glint in his eyes. He had deep, mysterious brown eyes.

'You know, of course, that I am the devil? You have just said that you love the devil.'

'No you are not the devil. You are the god of woodlands and countryside. There is no evil in you.'

'Did not the early church take me as a model for the devil? Look at my cloven hooves, my shaggy legs, and the horns on my forehead.'

'The church turned all pagan gods and spirits into devils, fiends, and imps.'

'Was the church wrong then?'

'The church did it with the best of intentions from its own point of view. But it was wrong. The ancient gods are not necessarily devils.'[49]

Later, after attending a course conducted by Sir George Trevelyan, Crombie describes an experience of 'identification' with Pan.

He stepped behind me and then walked into me so that we became one and I saw the surroundings through his eyes. At the same time, part of me – the recording, observing part – stood aside. The experience was not a form of possession but of identification [that conclusion is open to question]. The moment he stepped into me, the woods became alive with myriads of beings – elementals, nymphs, dryads, fauns, elves, gnomes, fairies – far too numerous to catalogue.[50]

One of these beings spoke to Crombie on the issue of ecology:

Man, we have no understanding of you. You upset the balance of nature, destroy the animals, turn land into desert, cut and burn the large trees, maim the landscape, blasting great wounds in the hills and mountains, slashing the living earth so that it will not heal. You pollute everything beneath you and everything above you. Everywhere you go is fouled and destroyed. Are you so stupid that you cannot realize you are destroying yourself? You cannot destroy us, for we are immortal and indestructible. But we care about this planet, we love it, it is our home and abode. It was once beautiful. Can you blame us if we consider you a parasite on the face of the Earth?[51]

Pan told Crombie that a wild area should be left for the nature spirits in the Findhorn garden. The community obliged. Crombie stressed that,

it is important for the future of mankind that belief in the Nature Spirits and their god Pan is re-established and that they are seen in their true light and not misunderstood. These beings, in spite of the innumerable outrages man has committed against nature, are only too pleased to help him if he will seek and ask for their co-operation. They must be believed in with complete sincerity and faith. They must never be taken for granted and should be given love and thanks for the work they do. With such co-operation, what could be achieved would seem miraculous to many. It has been sought and asked for at Findhorn, and the results have been given.[52]

Following that line would, in fact, lead people concerned for conservation to open themselves to demonic influences which, although described as wholesome, would do immense spiritual damage to the individuals involved.

Many people visit Findhorn because of its amazing horticultural successes. Sir George Trevelyan visited and wrote his approval of all the community (including Dorothy Maclean and Robert Crombie) stand for.[53] Not unnaturally, the Soil Association was also very impressed. But the community eventually realised that their experience with plants was meant to lead them on to having life-changing effects on humans.

David Spangler sees Findhorn as having done what, as yet, no other group has ever done – to sound 'the first note of what will be a "mass planetary initiation"'.[54]

The Myth of Findhorn is the Myth of Creation, of a rebirth of man emerging into a totally new consciousness. The myth is not a few individuals gaining a higher understanding of the spiritual and cosmic principles behind life and creation, but a period when the planet as one shall begin to strip away the old personality patterns, the old thought forms, prejudices and neuroses that distort the collective psyche, and in its place reveal the true divine nature of the planet.[55]

He continues: 'Findhorn's value is to demonstrate in practice the reality of New Age consciousness.'[56]

Conclusion

The Green Revolution has been perhaps the most dynamic change in Western society during the 1980s, even though it may partly have been caused by alarmist predictions. Ecology is, however, a biblical responsibility but has been neglected by Christians. So the New Age Ecology is taking over. Whether it be the moderate view voiced by the likes of Jonathon Porritt, the earth mysticism of the Gaia Hypothesis, or the strange world of Devas, nature spirits and Pan experienced at Findhorn, one thing is clear. All see conservation as a religious matter. It is one of the most powerful influences leading people into the New Age movement.

7

The World Conspiracy Theory

One of Sir Harry Secombe's songs is entitled 'If I ruled the world'. The song declares what good things the singer would provide for every boy and every girl. The song is an expression of man's dreaming and fantasy. But what if someone really did intend to take over the world? The New Age raises just such a question. Is it involved in an international conspiracy to take over the world? Is there a political plot or even a Satanic scheme with this objective? These are not questions merely of man's dreams, but of man's planning for the future well-being of future destruction of the world.

Such ideas seem to be a long way from the everyday world of shopping at the supermarket, going to the Saturday football match, or worrying about the future of the children. Why do they arise?

We have seen that the New Age is an international network of many different groups, encompassing the occult, Eastern religions and Western humanism. We have also seen that the New Age is concerned for the future peace, preservation and well-being of the world. The New Age is drawing more and more men and women from different backgrounds together on the grounds of common assumptions and objectives. So the question is posed. Is there a secret 'old-boy' network operating through such people in the world? Is it right merely to think of the New Age as an association of like-minded people seeking strength and fellowship with one another, or is there really an active and aggressive conspiracy at work to take over the world? At its simplest – and more foul – is Someone planning to take over this world?

We need to assemble and examine the arguments in favour and against this possibility, assess them in the light of Christian teaching, and then draw our own conclusions.

Arguments in Favour of a World Conspiracy

These arguments are, by and large, based on trends in the modern world, and on the teaching of particular individuals. For example, today's world is moving rapidly from the Industrial Age into the Information Age. We are all familiar with TV coverage of world events and crises by means of satellite. We send information around the world at virtually the speed of light through computers, Fax machines, and the latest inventions of man. We are becoming increasingly international, interdependent, and interrelated. What happens on the Stock Market in Japan, or Hong Kong will affect New York, and the financial welfare of American or British business within a few hours.

Against this background, Marilyn Ferguson, one of the names associated with the World Conspiracy Theory, claims that there are tens of thousands of 'entry points' serving to band together the like-minded in the New Age movement. Networking is achieved through conferences, phone-calls, air travel, books, phantom organisations, papers, pamphleteering, photocopying, lectures, workshops, parties, grapevines, mutual friends, summit meetings, coalitions, tapes and newsletters.[1]

What became public in the 1960s was, however, present in some form long before. Likewise, the seeds of New Age: Alice Bailey's 'Plan', the teaching that a new Messiah would one day appear, and the world conspiracy theory go back to 1844. That was the year when Helena Blavatsky founded the Theosophical Movement in America. She was greatly influenced by demonic spirits, and deeply involved in spiritism. Through her demon masters, Helena

Blavatsky was given a detailed plan (often referred to as 'The Plan') for the ordering of the world in the last days, and for the coming into the world of the Antichrist. Helena Blavatsky was commanded to keep the plan secret for a hundred years, and by and large this held good until 1975.

'After her death the Theosophical Movement was led by Alice (Ann) Bailey (1880–1949). In addition to bringing up a family on a shoe-string, she was also a prolific writer on the New Age.' In her books she set out a plan for a new world religion. She hated orthodox Christianity intensely, and became increasingly attracted to occultism and Eastern mysticism. Alice Bailey founded the 'Lucifer Trust' in New York to publish and promote her works. Later, the name of the trust was changed to 'Lucis Trust' and set up in London. That trust was described in one of Britain's popular women's magazines, *Options*, in a special article on 'New Age London' in November 1989: 'The Lucis Trust is an umbrella organisation that comes close to being the heart of the New Age. Its "World Goodwill" promotes right human relations globally and is represented at the United Nations, while "Triangles" comprises units of three people who link in thought and prayer to create a worldwide network.'[2]

Personal investigation of the Lucis Trust proved the claim in *Options* about it to be only too true. I was invited to send for a correspondence course giving training for discipleship for living in today's world – based on occult meditation, study and self-initiated service. I could send for any of Alice Bailey's twenty-four books of esoteric teaching planned to precede and condition the New Age, and I could also send for any of their 'Occasional Papers and Related Publications' associated with the theme of 'World Goodwill'. These were by such varied speakers and writers as David Spangler, Robert Muller, Fritjof Capra, Jonathon Porritt, the Archbishop of Canterbury and HRH The Prince of Wales.

Such New Age organisations can be found almost anywhere. A New Age *Directory for a New World* lists no fewer than 10,000 organisations, such as centres of various occult, Eastern and mystical religions, health food stores, metaphysical books stores, yoga teachers, etc., which they claim are linked or infiltrated in some way, or are being used to further New Age teaching. This is sure evidence that there is some real substance in the claim that there is a Plan.

Basilea Schlink, of the German Sisterhood of Mary, writes that the main political goal for the New Age movement is global control: 'The dissolution and/or destruction of individual nation states in the interests of peace and conservation are openly advocated.'[3]

While world domination appears from this to be the eventual goal, there seem to be various intermediate goals of a political, social and economic nature. For example, there are hopes and plans to have a universal credit card system, a world food authority that would control the world's food supply, a universal tax, the establishment of a world economic system, the recognition of biological controls on a worldwide basis of population and disease, and a minimum standard of freedom and welfare throughout the world.[4]

Against such a background, we shall not be surprised to learn that key figures in world politics are thought to be linked in some way with the past or the present of the New Age. Some have wondered whether the former Secretary-General of the United Nations, U. Tant, was associated with the New Age. It is generally agreed that Robert Muller, who has served the United Nations for more than thirty years, latterly in the post of Assistant Secretary-General, is a New Age activist.

Again, a man like David Spangler, a board member of Planetary Initiative (an organisation dedicated to the transformation of the world through political action) has been much influenced by Alice Bailey's writing, and writes and speaks of Lucifer as, 'in a sense the angel of man's inner evolution, who has a positive role in advancing humanity's cosmic consciousness'.[5]

Another name, and another witness to support the

possibility of a world conspiracy is that of Marilyn Ferguson, who is linked with the so-called Aquarian Conspiracy.

As we saw in the first chapter, the New Age regards the change from the age of Pisces, to the age of Aquarius as important. Devotees of the New Age are convinced that the world is about to be transformed by a newly-discovered human power derived from tapping into the supernatural. What this means in practice is spelt out for us by Marilyn Ferguson in her book *The Aquarian Conspiracy* (1980). All the activities involve an increased 'consciousness of one's consciousness, and a rethinking of one's fundamental understanding of reality'. Among the range of activities that Ferguson lists are the following: biofeedback – a technique using devices that permit the individual to monitor and regulate his or her own brain waves; creative activities such as painting and sculpting; self-help groups such as AA (Alcoholics Anonymous) or Overeaters Anonymous which stress 'higher powers' that must be consulted; hypnosis and self-hypnosis; all types of meditation: Zen, Tibetan Buddhist; types of yoga; exploration into one's dream life; interest in Jungian analysis; interest in martial arts, etc.[6]

Just as the New Age movement is composed of numerous strands of thought which diverge as well as converge, so the possibilities of world conspiracy theories have similar characteristics. Sometimes such theories appear to be majoring upon the development of the inner self; sometimes upon political or social movements; sometimes they are linked with well known names; sometimes they are movements of thought rather than of action.

In their book *The Todd Phenomenon*, authors Hick and Lewis sum the situation up. The various theories, they say:

agree on one thing. Someone is conspiring to rule the world. The conspiracy has been identified as [deriving from] communism, the illuminati, neo-Nazism, the Mafia, the Rothchilds, international bankers, the Masons, the Catholic Church . . . The Council on Foreign Relations, the Rockefellers, the Tri-

Lateral Commission, occultism, Zionism, the Bildebergers, Satanism, etc. Some take the position that all of these are interconnected, highly organised and controlled by one master-mind, a political genius. When speaking of the conspiracy, it is good to known which conspiracy theory one is talking about.[7]

A similar point is made by Nesta Webster, one of the most influential conspiracy writers, in her book *World Revolution*. She isolates five powers that support a world conspiracy: Grand Orient Masonry; Theosophy; pan-Germanism; international finance and social revolution. Her work supports the contention that three bases are most often seen in world conspiracy theories, namely, extremist politics, usually of the right-wing variety, involvement or fascination with occult practices or esoteric spirituality, and religious prejudice, usually anti-semitic or anti-Christian in nature.[8]

Yet another writer who supports the conspiracy theory is Constance Cumbey, who has written an important book entitled *The Hidden Dangers of the Rainbow*. Her thesis can be summarised as follows: 'The conspiracy is a network of all the cults, political and humanitarian organisations, and of isolated groups. The conspiracy follows the writing of Alice Bailey "like a recipe". The antichrist who is to come is Lord Maitreya, a deity of Eastern and occultic lore. When he is announced, all the world will have to undergo a Luciferic initiation and receive his mark.'[9]

Who is Lord Maitreya? This naming of the Antichrist is explained more fully in a full-page advertisement which the New Age movement placed in newspapers in many countries in April 1982. They explained:

The Christ is now here . . . pointing the way out of our present crisis . . . He comes not to judge, but to aid and inspire . . . The world teacher is known as Lord Maitreya, known by Christians as the Christ. And as Christians await the Second Coming, so the Jews await the Messiah, the Buddhists the fifth Buddha, the Moslems the Imam Mahdi, and the Hindus await Krishna. These are all names for one individual. His presence in the world guarantees there will be no third world war. With his help, we will build a new world.[10]

Any consideration of a world conspiracy theory inevitably raises questions to which it is almost impossible to give any authoritative reply. For example, does the New Age herald a movement towards world government? We can only reply that we see all the signs of such a movement – for example, the present day re-grouping of powers in East and West – but there is no clear evidence that this is the initiative of New Age. Some would claim that such a world figure as President Gorbachev is influenced by New Age ideals in his political ambitions, but where is the evidence to support such a claim? Again, people ask whether the New Age movement – or more correctly the convergence of New Age thinking – is a preparation for a world religion and the appearing of the Antichrist, spoken of in the New Testament.

While I want to comment on biblical prophecy later, let me make the point that biblical prophecy, in both Old and New Testament, which is foretelling the future, assures us that God has the future in his sovereign knowledge and will. God warns us of what will come, and asks that we be alert. We should, however, be cautious about categorically stating that particular world events or patterns are now fulfilling biblical prophecy. As with the first coming of Christ, we shall know when it happens.

I have sought to be open to the possibility that there is a world conspiracy. I have quoted from original sources, and I have tried to build a strong case. At times I have almost persuaded myself that what these people wrote is true – that the ultimate goal of New Age is world domination. If you have been thus persuaded, I would ask you to consider the Christian position, and also the arguments against a world conspiracy theory.

Arguments Against a World Conspiracy

We must be clear that while there are many international organisations and alliances – such as bankers, the Masonic movement, the Roman Catholic Church and the Anglican Communion – that does not of itself imply a conspiracy. High levels of activity are natural for like-minded people and groups. This is nothing new. Christians work together to further the kingdom of God. Communists aim to expand their control. It is natural that people linked with a common ideology will seek to implement a common agenda. That doesn't imply that the New Age movement has adopted a conspiracy to rule the world.

There can be networks of people who have common goals, but who do not accept and adhere to a common strategy. There may be many groups whose ideas and ideals overlap at some points and sharply differ at others. Groups may work together on some topics and work against exactly the same people on others.

A key word for the New Age is 'transformation', that is transformation of men from within, and mankind's environment from without. This would suggest that the New Age does not aim to control the world for political fulfilment, but to change man and his society. Nevertheless New Age and politics appear to be linked. If we can understand what that link is, then we shall better understand that there need not be a politically-motivated world conspiracy.

Douglas Groothuis, in his book *Unmasking the New Age*, makes the point that religion can never be severed from politics. Political vision stems from our deepest beliefs concerning reality and value; politics follows faith. As Groothius comments: 'It is not surprising then that the New Age has a political agenda or that the One is being taken to the streets, into political caucuses, before the halls of civil government and into the ballot box.'[11] While that is clearly true in the United States, it is increasingly true elsewhere. New Age politics, for example, are gaining ground in such places as Sweden. The Swedish Government has sponsored a conference attended by more than 500 people called 'Living companies in the New Age'. The Government-run Secretariat for Future Studies serves as an ongoing catalyst for implementing New Age ideas.[12]

Again, it is clear that the New Age has worldwide (and essential) concerns such as ecology, and the conservation of natural fuels and energy. But that does not mean or imply that the New Age wishes to control these matters, or that there is a world conspiracy in motion. Change is not control. Transformation of the world is not the same as the supposed triumph of the Antichrist.

The arguments, whether or not there is a world conspiracy, are strong on both sides. I believe that it is virtually impossible to settle the matter if we view the issues solely from a human point of view. However, if we begin to view history from another perspective – that of God – and review not only the past and the present, but also preview the future, we shall discover that there is a 'power encounter' and conflict between the God who made the world, and the god, or gods, of this world. I now turn, therefore, to consider the Christian view of the future.

The Christian View of the Future

Writing to the church at Ephesus, Paul spoke of God's plan for mankind from 'before the foundation of the world' to 'the fullness of time' (Ephesians 1:4, 10, RSV). The apostle has an overall view in which he sees that God is working his purposes out as year succeeds year.

The Bible records that account for us. God created man. Man sinned and rebelled against God. God planned to rescue and save mankind. He chose a nation, and from them he chose the Messiah. The Old Testament contains the history of mankind's sinful rebellion and is the record of God's saving purposes. After all the ups and downs of Old Testament history the promises of the coming Messiah are finally fulfilled when the Christ is born.

Many who attend Christmas carol services and midnight communions will be familiar with this part of the Christian revelation. Thousands who have listened to the carol services televised and broadcast from King's College, Cambridge, will at least be familiar with the words of the bidding prayer: 'Therefore let us read and mark in Holy Scripture the tale of the loving purpose of God from the first days of our disobedience unto the glorious redemption brought us by this Holy Christ. And let us make this place glad with our carols of praise.'

We must pause to consider one incident during the first days of our disobedience. Genesis chapter 11 records the story of the attempts of men to build the Tower of Babel from the earth to reach up to heaven. Man was seeking to reach up to God, and to govern the world. God confounded the languages of the world as a sign of his judgment and as a demonstration of his power that man apart from God could not govern the world.

When we come to the New Testament, we find Satan seeking to deceive Christ, and to claim authority to control the world. '"All these I will give you, if you will fall down and worship me" he says, inviting Jesus to survey his power and kingdom. "Begone, Satan! [comes the reply] for it is written, 'You shall worship the Lord your God, and Him only shall you serve'"' (Matthew 4:8–10, RSV).

The Bible is not only the record of God's restoration and forgiveness of sinful man, but also the demonstration of the power struggle and encounter between Jesus and Satan: the conflict between good and evil, right and wrong; the battle between the kingdom of God, and the kingdom of Satan. That battle was decisively fought and won when Jesus died upon the cross of Calvary on the first Good Friday, and rose again on the first glorious Easter Day. The Bible is full of the triumph of Jesus over Satan and evil. The kingdoms of this world will become the kingdoms of our God and his Christ.

The triumph of Christ upon the cross will culminate in his return to this earth in all his glory and power. The Bible records not only the first coming of Christ in weakness at Christmas, but also the second coming of Christ in glory and majesty at the close of the age. That is the New Age, as we have already hinted, for the Christian. The New Testament echoes this truth again and again. One in thirteen verses, on average, records this hope.

But it is a truth that will be challenged. The New Testament speaks about the coming of the 'man of lawlessness' (2 Thessalonians 2:3, NIV). We are told that the Lord Jesus Christ will not return until the rebellion occurs and the man of lawlessness is revealed, the man doomed to destruction. He opposes and exalts himself over everything that is called God or is worshipped; he even sets himself up in God's temple, proclaiming himself to be God:

> . . . the secret power of lawlessness is already at work; but the one who now holds it back will continue to do so till he is taken out of the way. And then the lawless one will be revealed, whom the Lord Jesus will overthrow with the breath of his mouth and destroy by the splendour of his coming. The coming of the lawless one will be in accordance with the work of Satan displayed in all kinds of counterfeit miracles, signs and wonders, and in every sort of evil that deceives those who are perishing. They perish because they refused to love the truth and so be saved. For this reason God sends them a powerful delusion so that they will believe the lie, and so that all will be condemned who have not believed the truth but have delighted in wickedness.
>
> (2 Thessalonians 2:7–12, NIV)

St John also teaches about the coming of the Antichrist (1 John 2:18–27) while Jesus himself warned his disciples of error and deceit and of people making false claims to be the Christ (Matthew 24:5, 23 and Mark 13:6, 21–22).

The Conclusion

Is there, then, a world conspiracy afoot? To what conclusion may we come? It can be argued that a conspiracy, by its very nature, will be hidden if it is effective. However, we can affirm the following.

First, God is the God of history, and his victory and triumph will ultimately be made clear. His kingdom, for which we pray, and which was clearly established through the death, resurrection and ascension of Jesus Christ, will come on earth as it is now in heaven. However, that kingdom and power is challenged directly by Satan and all his evil hosts. It is also indirectly opposed by all who do not submit to the rule of Christ, and who say that 'we will not have this man to reign over us' (Luke 19:14). Although the New Age does not have all the usual manifestations of a movement – no central organisation, no headquarters, no hierarchy, no creed – yet it is an unholy alliance throughout the world challenging the rule and authority of God.

Secondly, the New Age must be viewed as a very significant shift in mankind's world-view.

After the years of humanistic thought and secular materialism, it is recalling us to an awareness of the spiritual and the transcendent. That is good. What is not good and helpful is the fact that the spiritual to which we are called is false, incomplete and deceptive. We are called to a relative truth, and not to the unchanging truth about God and man. We are invited to embrace a faith in which man seeks to change himself, and improve himself. We are not presented with a Creator God who makes us, loves us, saves, and forgives us.

Thus the New Age, while claiming to offer the answers, reveals itself as morally and spiritually bankrupt and unfit to lead the world because it cannot assure mankind of whether the anticipated transformation will result in life becoming better or worse.

Thirdly, we must affirm that God is the Lord of history. We can see history unfolding in a straight line of events, and not repeating itself in a declining or increasing spiral of good or evil. The New Age has a cyclical view of history. The Western/Christian world has a linear view of history.

Fourthly, we are to affirm that it is for Jesus Christ that all things exist. He is the one who holds all things together (Colossians 1:15–19). It is Christ who holds the keys of the future. He has been given the keys of Death and Hades. He has within his hands the scroll of the future. Only he, as the Lamb that was slain, is worthy to open the books, to break the seals of future revelation, and to have power and might, and honour and glory ascribed to him. The future lies in the mystery and purposes of God.

The key to the future is not held in the hands of conspiring sinful men. Only God, and his Christ – not Satan, or some strange world figure and leader, yet to be revealed – holds the key to the future of the world and the destiny of mankind. The world plan that will succeed is not found in a theory in the minds of man, but revealed in the purposes of God, our creator, maker and King.

8

'Spiritual Powers' – Genuine and Counterfeit

The New Age movement is in many ways concerned with the *spiritual*. It recognises that there is far more to life than that which can be seen. But 'spiritual' can mean many things, and can include both good and evil powers. How can we distinguish between these?

Many Christians say that those phenomena which are *from God* are 'genuine' whereas others are 'counterfeit'. If the Bible refers to 'counterfeit miracles, signs and wonders' (2 Thessalonians 2:9, NIV), then the genuine article must be available *somewhere*. In addition, the counterfeit must resemble the genuine in many respects in order to deceive: after all, no forger would try to manufacture a counterfeit thirteen-pound note because there is no 'genuine' thirteen-pound note; instead, forged ten-pound notes are made to resemble the original in as many details as possible.

We have a problem in distinguishing *spiritual causes* because they are *unseen*, whereas all we can see are their *physical effects*. For example, the Bible refers to Peter and Paul having trances when God gave them significant visions (Acts 10:10 and 22:17). However, that does not mean that the trances of spiritualist mediums are also caused by God. The trances in themselves are *neutral*: they are simply the physical side-effects on the body when there is an intense focus of attention on whatever is taking place in the spiritual realm.[1]

The physical side-effects associated with 'supernatural'

messages do not necessarily show us what caused these effects. Perhaps the human ability to receive information from 'spiritual' sources could be likened to a television set. We might say that there are a variety of 'channels' or 'broadcasting stations' but all of them are projected on to the screen in the same manner.

The Test by Contents

How, then, can we discern between the different sources? Just as different television stations broadcast different programmes, so the *content* of spiritual messages indicates their *character* and *origin*. This was the major test used by the early Church:

> . . . no-one who is speaking by the Spirit of God says, 'Jesus be cursed' and no-one can say, 'Jesus is Lord,' except by the Holy Spirit.
>
> (1 Corinthians 12:3, NIV)

> This is how you can recognise the Spirit of God: Every spirit that acknowledges that Jesus Christ has come in the flesh is from God, but every spirit that does not acknowledge Jesus is not from God.
>
> (1 John 4:2–3, NIV)

In the same way, the validity of Old Testament prophecy was to be tested through its *content*:

> If a prophet, or one who foretells by dreams, appears among you . . . and . . . says, 'Let us follow other gods' (gods you have not known) 'and let us worship them,' you must not listen to the words of that prophet or dreamer . . . That prophet or dreamer must be put to death, because he preached rebellion against the Lord your God . . .
>
> (Deuteronomy 13:1–5, NIV)

It should be noted that these three biblical quotations focus on the *Lordship* and *person* of Jesus, and on the strict biblical instructions not to worship any other 'gods' except Yahweh. These principles exclude 'New Age' teachings which promote pantheism (the idea that 'All is God'), syncretism (the teaching that all religions are one) or monism (the idea that 'All is One'). In addition, these biblical tests rule out all teachings which deny the existence of a personal god or which claim that Jesus is not the only Messiah.

Another test refers to predictive prophecy, which I shall discuss further in the next chapter:

> You may say to yourselves, 'How can we know when a message has not been spoken by the Lord?' If what a prophet proclaims in the name of the Lord does not take place or come true, that is a message the Lord has not spoken. That prophet has spoken presumptuously.
>
> (Deuteronomy 18:21–22, NIV)

Owing to the danger of a prophet speaking 'presumptuously', St Paul gave instructions to the church in Corinth that: 'Two or three prophets should speak, and the others should weigh carefully what is said' (1 Corinthians 14:29, NIV).

The Gift of Discernment

Why should the others 'weigh carefully what is said'? I believe that they need to be using the ability to distinguish between spirits mentioned in 1 Corinthians 12:10. It is important for all prophecies to be tested. There is the possibility that somebody can become carried away by personal emphases or eccentricities, and 'prophesy' in God's name what actually comes from human or even demonic sources. In some of these cases, there might seem to be no doctrinal error and there might also be no future prediction to check. However, the Spirit of God may give insights to others, showing that this revelation is not truly from God.[2]

The gift of discernment can also refer to the ability to see evil spirits which are affecting or influencing someone. In the experience of one Christian lady, the spirits are seen in a variety of ways:

> Different spirits appear in different forms. Perversion is like a crocodile – I know it well because I've dealt with it on two occasions. On a homosexual prostitute it had a greenish, long snout; usually I can see the eyes . . .
> Spirits of affliction usually look like a black lump on a person, like a small animal clinging to a person . . .[3]

The Test by Effects

Another test of the *source* of a spiritual revelation is the *effect* which it produces. This is much less easy to document. To return to the example of a television, it is often argued that the frequent watching of violence on television tends to make people express their fantasised violence in actual real-life situations. This might be so, but it is difficult to prove. There might be an association in general terms, but not everyone who watches violent programmes automatically becomes a violent criminal. In the same way, exposure to various kinds of spiritual phenomena might produce effects which can be seen statistically even if they are not present in each and every person.

In 1986 I interviewed a random sample of 108 nurses in Leeds, West Yorkshire, about their 'supernatural' or 'spiritual' experiences. Each interview also included a widely-used test for measuring 'psychological well-being'.[4] Other studies in the USA and Britain had shown that people reporting certain kinds of spiritual experiences ranked significantly higher than average on this scale of psychological well-being. However, this result was produced by the very high rankings of a minority whose experiences seem to have been those of the presence of God. The American sociologists Greeley and McCready noticed this effect on their results and called it 'the twice-born factor'.[5]

By contrast, I discovered that those who had ever been involved in trying to contact the dead through spiritualism ranked *lower* than average on this scale of psychological well-being. The following table compares the thirteen nurses whose principal spiritual experience was that of the 'presence of God' with the fifteen nurses who had ever been involved in spiritualism. In between are the eighty other nurses who reported other kinds of 'supernatural' experiences, or else none at all.[6]

Table 1

TYPE OF 'SUPERNATURAL' EXPERIENCE	PSYCHOLOGICAL WELL-BEING SCORE [Highest = 9, Lowest = 1]
'Presence of God' group	5.9
All others	5.7
Spiritualist involvements group	4.6

This difference is statistically significant.[7]

The same pattern also emerged from less objective self-assessments of personal 'happiness' or 'satisfaction with life'. All the nurses independently ranked their own 'satisfaction with life' on a ten-point scale. This was done near the beginning of the interview, before the later discussions on spiritual experiences. However, on average, the 'presence of God' group reported higher than average levels of personal happiness whereas those who had ever been involved in spiritualism gave noticeably lower self-assessments.

Again, a statistically highly significant pattern emerged from questions on donations to charity, but this was because some of the 'presence of God' group gave away at least ten per cent of their income. A better guide to generosity among nurses comes from blood donations, which are not so directly influenced by religious doctrines.[8] Nevertheless, the same pattern still emerged when comparing all those who had *never even tried* to give their blood for the benefit of others.[9] These results are summarised in Table 2.

Therefore, it is clear than an involvement in spiritualism is associated with reduced levels of psychological well-being, lower levels of expressed 'happiness', and less generous attitudes towards others. The opposite effect is associated with experiences of the presence of God. Those reporting other kinds of 'supernatural' experiences, or none, tend to be in the middle, between these two groups.

These findings are consistent with the test by *results* advocated by Jesus for distinguishing between true and false prophets:

> They come to you in sheep's clothing, but inwardly they are ferocious wolves. By their fruit you will recognise them. Do people pick grapes from thornbushes, or figs from thistles? Likewise every good tree bears good fruit, but a bad tree bears bad fruit.
>
> (Matthew 7:15–17, NIV)

Other Kinds of Effects

In a similar manner, St Paul contrasted the difference between the 'acts of the sinful nature', such as 'sexual immorality . . . idolatry and witchcraft: hatred [etc.],' and what he describes as 'the fruit of the [Holy] Spirit' which is expressed in 'love, joy, peace, patience . . . [etc.]' (Galatians 5:19–23, NIV).

'Witchcraft', linked here to idolatry, refers to the worship or service of spiritual powers which are hostile to God. Closely related to it is the consultation of the dead through mediums. God's people were given strict instructions not to become involved in such activities. For example:

> Do not practise divination or sorcery . . . Do not turn to mediums or seek out spiritists, for you will be defiled by them.
>
> (Leviticus 19:26, 31, NIV)

Table 2

TYPE OF 'SUPERNATURAL' EXPERIENCE		'HAPPINESS'	GENEROSITY	NEVER OFFERED BLOOD
	Highest =	10	6	
	Lowest =	1	1	
'Presence of God' group		7.5	4.8	23%
All others		7.1	2.8	32.5%
Spiritualist involvements group		6.5	2.5	46%

> Let no-one be found among you who sacrifices his son or
> daughter in the fire, who practises divination or sorcery, inter-
> prets omens, engages in witchcraft, or casts spells, or who is a
> medium or spiritist or who consults the dead. Anyone who does
> these things is detestable to the Lord.
>
> (Deuteronomy 18:10–12, NIV)

Among my random sample of 108 nurses, thirty-eight
had been involved with either spiritualism or the use of
Ouija boards; a further twenty-one had consulted some
other kind of professional fortune-teller. In modern Britain
there are many people who have become involved to a
lesser or greater extent with activities of this nature. There
are also some who are involved in the worship of Satan,
'black magic' and witch covens; among some of these
groups it appears that child sacrifice is currently being
practised.[10]

Often those who become involved in séances or Ouija
boards are initially attracted out of curiosity. At first they
may express doubts or scepticism, but during the séance
itself they might become aware of feelings of fear, coldness,
or what they sense to be an evil presence. The following
detailed account from a twenty-four-year-old nurse is representative:

> We went to a séance – nine of us, boys and girls. It was
> organised by the parents of one of the girls. She'd dabbled in
> this sort of thing before and considered herself an expert in
> getting across to the other side. It was organised in the girl's
> living room. The curtains were pulled, they dimmed the lights,
> put hands on the table. She called up a 'messenger' between the
> two sides – a 'bridge' between our side and their side. Nearly all
> of us were disbelieving until it went really cold in the room
> (though the central heating was on) and all of us got the shakes.
> It was not the cold of being frightened. I had a really dry feeling
> in my throat. I was aware that my eyes were burning – like when
> I'm frightened; I felt clammy. It makes heckles rise in me now
> to talk about it.
>
> It's as though the light definitely seemed to change – I don't

know if it was a reaction of my eyes dilating. I wanted to leave the room but a morbid curiosity welded me to the chair.

I felt some presence in the room. One of the girls recognised this and spoke to it. It ended when one of the boys got up and left the room and put the lights on. It shook me up for the rest of the evening – and also now, thinking about it. Now I don't disbelieve it but keep an open mind – but I wouldn't do it again.

That this experience affected her very deeply can be seen in its after-effects: she said,

The séance lasted about forty minutes but the effect lasted all of the evening and into the nighttime because I couldn't get to sleep, thinking of it. I was thinking about it for a lot of the following week . . . It was a long time before I could walk up the stairs without a light on. I needed a light to go to sleep. I got jittery walking home in the dark on my own: if I was on my own it made my mind flip back to the events of the séance. I was afraid of the dark for probably just a few months, about two months or so . . .

Other nurses described in more detail experiences, either at a séance or elsewhere, in which they had seen, heard, smelled, or otherwise become aware of, what they interpreted as the presence of dead people. One senior nurse told me how she had become involved in spiritualism at about the age of twenty-five. At one séance she witnessed what was described by the spiritualists as a 'transfiguration'. The male medium was 'dressed in black with a light on his face; his hair lengthened and shortened, went white or black, and his features changed'.

This is, however, very different from the Transfiguration of Jesus: 'His clothes became dazzling white, whiter than anyone in the world could bleach them. And there appeared before them Moses and Elijah, who were talking with Jesus . . . Then a cloud appeared and enveloped them, and a voice came from the cloud: "This is my Son, whom I love. Listen to him!"' (Mark 9:3–7, NIV). Peter, who was present at the time, described himself and his companions as 'eye-witnesses of his [Christ's] majesty', when Jesus 'received honour and glory from God the Father when the voice came to him from the Majestic Glory, saying, "This is my Son, whom I love; with him I am well pleased." We ourselves heard this voice that came from heaven when we were with him on the sacred mountain' (2 Peter 1:16–18, NIV).

Instead, the spiritualist so-called 'transfiguration' re-markably resembles the changed appearance of some people during Christian ministries of 'exorcism' or 'deliver-ance'. In cases in which a *person* (rather than a *place*) is particularly subject to demonic control or influence, the demon might manifest itself, among other ways, through bizarre facial contortions or speaking in the voice of a member of the opposite sex.[11] Similarly, ugly or horribly contorted expressions often appear on the faces of Muslims entering into trances during Islamic séances in which the demon is not expelled but is instead sought after for the social or physical benefits it is supposed to convey.[12]

Over one third of my random sample of 108 nurses spoke of experiences which they considered to be 'the presence of the dead'. For example, a twenty-seven-year-old nurse said:

> My grandfather died when I was twelve . . . on August the thirteenth, 1970, and I felt close to him. I feel he's watching over me and when I'm upset or else very happy (such as now being pregnant) I'd like to feel that he knows about this. I keep a photo of him . . .
>
> 'Guidance' is a better word, not necessarily 'presence'; he's just there. It's 'comfort' rather than 'influence'. I had a very traumatic year in 1979 when I . . . relied on him, though I don't know what the right word is: comforted, I suppose. During that time I felt he was there quite a lot.

Later in the interview she gave details of what happened during that 'traumatic two years':

> I've been married before, at eighteen, a big mistake . . . After eighteen months I met J, who I'm with now. He was married too . . . It was horrendous for two years, when I got a divorce

but J's wife wouldn't divorce him. We had to wait five years. We've been together six years . . . J and I bought a house together, then, five years ago and were living together before then . . . We'd prefer to be legally married for the child's sake, and will do that after the divorce is sorted out.

During this 'traumatic time', she became aware of the presence of what she identified as her grandfather:

I felt he was saying to me, 'You're not on your own' or 'Don't be frightened'. It comes as a strong mental intuition more than an audible voice, an inner feeling . . .

This nurse's awareness of this 'presence' stemmed from the time when her adulterous relationship led to the breaking up of two marriages. Among my sample of nurses in Leeds I also discovered a statistically significant link between experiences interpreted as 'the presence of the dead' and involvements with spiritualism or Ouija boards. Sometimes there might be a gap of a few years between the two events, but it seems as if the person becomes 'tuned in' to particular types of spiritual experience.

For example, the senior nurse who told me about a spiritualist 'transfiguration' also told me how, when she was twenty-nine years old, she twice saw an apparition of a lady closely resembling her grandmother. On the day following the second appearance, a patient awaiting a sex-change operation, who was also a medium, not only knew about what had occurred but also told the nurse that she had 'a Chinaman' on her shoulder. About twenty-five years later this 'Chinaman' was recognised to be an evil spirit and was commanded to depart in the name of Jesus. As a result of this she became a Christian. A few weeks later she noticed that a recurring ache on that shoulder (which she had previously attributed to a horse-riding accident) had suddenly disappeared.

A similar connection between demonic influences and physical ailments is described in several places in the New Testament (for example, Luke 13:10–13; Matthew

9:32–33; 12:22; 17:15–18). The common English term 'possession' is very misleading because the Greek term for 'demonisation' (*daimonizomai*) actually refers to a *range of influences from* or *activities by* evil spirits. Therefore many apparently 'normal' people, including nurses in responsible positions whom I interviewed, might be subject to the milder forms of demonic *influence*. Only in severe cases might it become expressed in forms which could be regarded as symptoms of psychological instability.

In one case reported to me, a professional medium had chosen to look for other forms of work. Then on her way to the employment exchange she felt the spirits telling her to return home. When she asked them why, they told her, '*We need you to work full-time for us – and if you don't, we'll put you into a mental asylum.*' She knew this was no vain threat, because she knew of other mediums who had suffered a similar fate. However, she was so scared by this experience that she prayed for God to deliver her from the spirits, which he did.

How can 'Healings' be Produced by Occult Practitioners?

Many people find it difficult to understand how spiritualist mediums and other occult practitioners can appear to produce healings if the agency involved is demonic. It appears to be a case of Satan driving out Satan (Matthew 12:26). Some Christians see the 'healings' as cases of 'counterfeit miracles' (2 Thessalonians 2:9; Mark 13:22). They further claim that the healings only serve to bring the person deeper under demonic control or influence.

In some cases, there might be 'natural' explanations for the healings. For example, medical doctors are familiar with what they call the 'placebo effect', when a patient is given an inert substance but believes it to be a powerful medicine. The psychological effect of taking the medicine can in itself produce some relief of symptoms, at least for a while. This is especially the case for those illnesses which are known to be 'psychosomatic' – that is, in which the illness is known to be influenced by mental states.

Some illnesses also run their course and the patient might be able to recover naturally, without the use of medicine. However, if some treatment had been given at the same time, the patient might think that the recovery was due to that treatment. In this way, various therapies continue to be used even when there is little or no scientific proof of their efficacy.

On the other hand, some folk medicines do contain drugs which have definite therapeutic effects. It was from an analysis of plants traditionally used by some of the native peoples of South America that quinine was first discovered by Western doctors.

Another explanation for apparent 'healings' in occult contexts involves some understanding of the ways in which demons might produce physical illnesses. There are cases in which a demon appears to be *'dormant'* in somebody and only manifests as physical illness at certain times. For example, a young woman was frequently prevented from attending church services by bouts of asthma which occurred just when she was about to go to church. She received healing after the cause was diagnosed as a *'spirit'* of asthma, from which she was delivered. Then other evil spirits began to manifest themselves. It seemed as if the evil spirits did not like going to church – but only one of them was needed to prevent this, without the others showing themselves. The symptoms of asthma were intermittent, as if the spirit had been 'dormant' for periods of time while it was still inside the girl's body.

Similarly, Bill Musk describes a Sudanese medium whose wife's legs had been severely burned in a kerosene accident and had been inadequately treated at the local hospital. One night as she slept, her husband began to intone strange words and make stroking movements over her. Then she began to speak in a deep, masculine voice – a symptom of demonisation. The demon was not cast out, but the next morning the woman's legs were greatly improved.[13]

On the basis of cases like these, I suspect that a medium might be able to produce apparent physical healing through the co-operation of the demon but *without the demon being expelled from the affected person's body*.

Revelations or Fraud? The Case of Doris Stokes

Many mediums claim to receive revelations from the spirit world. Sometimes these seem to be inexplicable in ordinary terms. However, scientific investigators who studied fourteen different mediums and psychics found that ninety per cent of their statements could have been taken from clues provided by their audience. Among the 'inexplicable' ten per cent of their statements, only one in ten actually turned out to be true! The scientists concluded that the one per cent which were both 'inexplicable' and 'true' could easily be explained away as due to chance alone.[14]

Another explanation is fraud. It is known, for example, that a number of spiritualist mediums travel around a regular circuit of meetings and can build up some knowledge about the regular congregation in each place.[15] A much more sophisticated kind of fraud has been revealed by journalists who investigated the claims of a famous medium named Doris Stokes whose books have been best-sellers, grossing more than £2 million.

In a report published in *The Mail on Sunday*, journalists John Dale and Richard Holliday showed how many of the details given in Doris Stokes's books are not facts but fabrications. For example, in her book *Voices in My Ear* Doris Stokes described how she was in a spiritualist meeting in Boston, Lincolnshire, when she was interrupted by the spirit of a man named Joe. She claimed Joe had just died in his sleep but did not realise it. Her account then states that, accompanied by others, she took the spirit to the Carpenter's Arms pub where the landlord did not know that Joe, his father, had died.

However, according to Mrs Madge Davis, the wife of the president of the spiritualist congregation in Boston:

> It is untrue that nobody knew of Joe's death. His body had been laid out for three or four days.
> It is untrue that nobody in the meeting knew this: a close woman friend of Joe's was sitting almost next to Doris.
> It is untrue that the landlord did not know of the death.
> It is untrue that Doris and others escorted the spirit through the streets.

Dale and Holliday also show how 'even her story about her son's death is wrong'. They quote her account of how she coped with events in Grantham after her five-month-old son, John Michael, died in 1945:

> I was standing at the mirror in the kitchen when the air raid sirens started . . . I heard the whistle of falling bombs and then there was the most appalling crash. My whole body jarred, the floor rocked under my feet, the mirror swung on the wall.
> As I stared at the strangely white face, I realised I didn't want to die.

However, according to War Office records, the last German raid on Grantham took place on 24th October 1942, *but John Michael Stokes died on 26th January 1945.*[16]

One of those who contacted the newspaper in response to this article was Mrs Janette O'Donnell, whose son, Gary, had died from a brain tumour just before his third birthday. Mrs O'Donnell described how, after a detailed telephone conversation, Doris Stokes gave her a personal invitation to one of her public performances. She also sent some complimentary tickets and a cheque to cover the train fare. At the meeting, Doris Stokes then announced that she was in contact with a dead child named Gary O'Donnell whose mother was in the audience, sitting in a certain row. The mother was asked to stand up, but was unable to say publicly that she had already told Doris Stokes all these details over the telephone.[17]

Demonic Powers

This is not to say that all kinds of 'supernatural' powers are really fraud. It is possible that certain 'supernatural' experiences are actually produced by demons. Some *might* even come from a 'natural' human sensitivity to the spiritual realm which in itself is neutral but can be used for either good or evil. However, in practice it is virtually impossible to distinguish any possible 'neutral' source from those which might be either demonic or divine.

For example, in Japan I met a man who claimed to be an 'amateur medium' and who reported various experiences involving contact with spirits of the dead. He thought that his powers were hereditary and told me how one of his sons could bend metal objects like Uri Geller. Through his influence, a number of new religious rites had been started in the factory with which he was closely connected. New cult objects for worship had also been set up in other factories belonging to the same firm.[18] In this case, there are close links between psychic powers and cults which, in St Paul's words, are directed 'to demons, not to God' (1 Corinthians 10:20, NIV).

It is interesting that *metal* objects, which are particularly conductive of electricity, are the ones which feature in Uri Geller-type 'spoon-bending'. In the same way, our modern age of electronics has revealed a new type of ailment among those who seem to have particular psychic 'powers' over computers, washing machines and other such devices. Such machines seem to malfunction simply because of being near to such individuals! What seems significant in this context, however, is that very often such people are also involved in spiritualism or other occult activities.[19] Might it be that their 'extra' electromagnetic 'sphere of influence', which extends wider than that of 'normal' individuals, is in fact produced by demonic presences which are closely associated with them?

In cases such as that of Doris Stokes, there may be fraud mixed in with occasional insights from demonic powers.

However, irrespective of whether her claimed 'revelations' actually came from demons or from fraud, her influence on people had the effect of leading at least some of them further into spiritualism. They might then have become subject to demonic bondages themselves. Therefore, even if the revelations by Doris Stokes were fraudulent, they still served the interests of the powers of darkness.

And was it merely 'coincidence', then, that after I had cited the articles exposing Doris Stokes the envelope containing those articles fell on to an electric fire while I was out of the room? It was singed and would have caught alight if I had returned just a few seconds later. Was this just 'coincidence' – or a form of demonic attack?

Perhaps I should have taken more heed of this incident and prayed for further protection. Later that same day I posted off what I had written; less than a minute later the front wheel of my bicycle inexplicably buckled and sent me headlong into the road. I thank God that no vehicles were passing at that moment.

John Wimber comments that Jesus rebuked the storm on the lake in the same way as he rebuked demons. He suggests that the powers of darkness were aware that Jesus was going to the other side of the lake, where he would meet the Gadarene demoniac (Mark 4:35–5:20). Therefore they tried to attack him physically in order, if possible, to kill him.

In the same way, we need to be aware of the spiritual battle which is involved when Christians confront the powers of darkness or expose their works. However, the one who is in us is greater than the one who is in the world (1 John 4:4). In the final chapter of this book Michael Cole will emphasise the necessity for every Christian to put on the full armour of God which is described in Ephesians 6:10–18.

As we engage in spiritual warfare, it is necessary to be equipped with the gifts of the Holy Spirit. Spiritualist mediums and others may seek to imitate some of these, but the 'genuine article' is to be found in the Christian Church. I shall discuss these further in the next chapter.

9

Is Christian 'Renewal' Really 'New Age' in Disguise?

'That sounds just like spiritualism' (referring to the use of 'words of knowledge' at one of John Wimber's conferences).

'This book says that all I'd thought was from God is really from secular psychology' (referring to Hunt and McMahon's book *The Seduction of Christianity*).[1]

'That's not biblical Christianity' (referring to a comet unpredicted by scientists but which was predicted by a Christian prophet in America).

These are three of the reactions which I have heard expressed about new trends in the Christian Church today. They are indicative of the kinds of reactions which some people have towards that which is new and unexpected. Others welcome these new trends as signs that God is renewing his Church.

Are these kinds of phenomena really derived from the occult, or from secular psychology, as some claim? Is modern Christianity being 'seduced' by the kinds of teachings and practices associated with the New Age movement? Or, are these genuine works of God which have been imitated by occult and New Age practitioners?

This chapter concentrates on the three areas illustrated above, namely 'words of knowledge', 'inner healing' and 'predictive prophecy'.

Words of Knowledge

In the New Testament this expression is used in 1 Corinthians 12:8 (AV) but no further explanation is given about what it means. Presumably this was because its meaning was sufficiently clear to St Paul's readers. Many people think the term refers to 'supernatural' insights and revelations about others, because several examples of these are provided elsewhere in the Bible. These include:

(i) Samuel's knowledge about Saul's errand and the finding of his father's donkeys (1 Samuel 9:19–20).

(ii) Elisha's knowledge of Gehazi's deceit and of the king of Aram's plans (2 Kings 5:26; 6:9–12).

(iii) Christ's descriptions of Nathanael under the fig-tree and of the Samaritan woman's past life (John 1:48–51; 4:16–19).

(iv) Peter's discernment of the deception in Ananias and Sapphira (Acts 5:1–11).

There are other examples which are not so obvious, even though the stories are very familiar. For instance, in Luke 19:5, did Jesus already know the name of Zacchaeus by 'natural' means, or did the information come 'supernaturally'? Simon the Pharisee, in Luke 7:39, certainly thought that one sign of a prophet was the ability to recognise what was in people's hearts; Jesus showed that he knew not only about the kind of woman who was at his feet but also about Simon's thoughts: 'He did not need man's testimony about man, for he knew what was in a man' (John 2:25).

However, this gift was by no means restricted to the divine Son of God who also took on human limitations, because similar giftings were apparent also in Samuel, Elisha and Peter, among others. In some instances the information about others' past or present circumstances is expressed in a prophetic manner:

. . . Elizabeth was filled with the Holy Spirit. In a loud voice she exclaimed: 'Blessed are you among women, and blessed is the child you will bear! But why am I so favoured, that the mother of my Lord should come to me? . . . Blessed is she who has believed that what the Lord has said to her will be accomplished!'

(Luke 1:41–45, NIV)

Today, cases of these sorts of revelations have been interpreted in a variety of ways, according to the presuppositions of different Christians. Three contrasting views are as follows:

(i) Bishop David Pytches believes these to be examples of divine revelation. In his book *Does God Speak Today?* he provides many more examples.[2]

(ii) Morton Kelsey, an Episcopalian priest and Jungian psychologist, takes as his starting point the evidence for 'extra-sensory perception' (ESP). He then interprets biblical references to supernatural revelations as further examples of the same kind.[3]

(iii) Dr Peter Masters, minister at the Metropolitan Tabernacle in London, draws a sharp line between supernatural revelations in the Bible and those experienced today. He regards the former as divine, but sees the latter as examples of occult 'clairvoyance', which he describes as 'disobedient to God's word and highly dangerous'.[4]

Masters's church and the occasional publication which he edits were founded in the nineteenth century by C. H. Spurgeon, so it is ironic that David Pytches should cite Spurgeon himself as using 'words of knowledge'! On a number of occasions Spurgeon pointed to somebody present in the hall and described their situations very accurately, without having any 'natural' knowledge of the person. For example, once Spurgeon pointed out a man in the crowd, a shoemaker whose shop was open on Sundays, saying: 'It was open last Sunday morning; he took ninepence and there was fourpence profit out of it . . .' The shoemaker knew that these details were accurate and that they could only have been known through a revelation from God. He became a Christian as a result.[5]

This is one among many examples of highly specific 'words of knowledge'. Their use in healing contexts has become popularised by John Wimber, an American pastor. Sometimes they are used to bring forward for prayer those people whom, it is believed, God wants to heal. In 1986, at a conference in Harrogate, England, Wimber announced one night that he believed God wanted them to demonstrate on the stage how to pray for healing. In order to do so, he wanted God to reveal very clearly which people he wanted to come forward. After prayer, he announced,

> There's a woman named Janet who at eleven years of age had a minor accident that's proven to be a problem throughout her adult life. It had something to do with an injury to her tailbone but now it's caused other kinds of problems and so there's radiating pain that comes down over her – er – lower back and down over her backside and down her legs. It has something to do with damage to a nerve but it also has to do with some sort of a functional problem with the – um – I think it's called the sacro-iliac.

There was indeed someone who matched this description exactly. She was in the overflow hall down the road, where she received prayer for healing. Over a year later she wrote to me: 'My back appears healed and I am not receiving any discomfort from it.'[6]

Elsewhere I have analysed this example and worked out the statistical probabilities of correctly guessing all these features by chance alone. I found that the chances against accurately diagnosing *all* these various details by chance alone were at least three million to one.[7]

In my study of Wimber's conferences I could find no evidence of fraud. The conferences were advertised in popular Christian magazines and organised by different groups of local Christians who had no control over those who might apply to attend. Those registering came from all over Britain, or even further afield, with no previous personal contact with Wimber or his team from the USA. Some British Christians have also formed part of such teams but there is no evidence of 'spies' providing information about people who are then described in public words of knowledge.

The example given above is one among many cases of highly specific information conveyed through 'words of knowledge'. This is in stark contrast to the kinds of results obtained by conventional tests for ESP. They do obtain statistically significant results but have had to do so by limiting the number of possible choices to a known, predetermined set. This is in order to calculate the statistical probabilities of random guesses. For example, subjects for testing might be asked to tell which card has been chosen or to predict which light will flash out of a limited possible set. The results of hundreds of such series are then tabulated and analysed for statistical significance. Even the 'best' scores in such trials have an accuracy level well below 100 per cent, such as scores of 2,923 out of 11,000 trials or 466 out of 1,600 trials. In these examples, the 'intrinsic percentage score' (when adjusted for discrepancies with statistical probability etc.) are 8.2 per cent and 11.4 per cent respectively.[8]

Perhaps because of the relatively 'boring' nature of such experiments, even individuals producing what are very significant scores statistically (such as 270 out of 950, compared with a chance expectation of 190) have sooner or later lost their abilities.[9]

Nevertheless, there still remains some evidence that human beings are able to obtain *certain* kinds of information in ways which lie beyond those of our ordinary senses. Although categories can at times blur into each other, several types of ESP are commonly distinguished:

Telepathy involves communication between minds other than by the known senses, usually understood to occur at the same point in time.

Clairvoyance involves the mental perception of what is normally 'out of sight', whether hidden by space or by time.

Clairaudience is similar to clairvoyance but involves 'hearing' rather than 'seeing'.

Telekinesis involves the movement of physical objects without touching them, as in certain 'poltergeist' phenomena or Uri Geller's spoon-bending.

An obvious common factor is that these experiences occur to *people*. It is clear that human beings do have a *capacity* for 'spiritual' experiences and that this appears to be part of their very humanity. Christians need to ask why this is so. If we believe that God created mankind with this capacity and that originally this was deemed to be 'very good', then we have to assume that God's purpose in creating man this way was in order for humanity to experience *God*. However, as a result of human sin this potential has often been used for the wrong purposes, through 'tuning in' to spiritual forces which are opposed to God. Because these wrong uses are so widespread, we might mistakenly assume that they came first, and that the Christian equivalents are copied from the occult forms, instead of the other way round. *Methods* or *channels* might in themselves be *neutral* but can become means by which information from extra-human sources might be obtained.

It is possible that there *might* be a latent awareness or ability within humans and other forms of life which in itself is neither divine nor demonic. However, in practice it seems to be very commonly associated with 'spiritual' contexts, whether in Christianity or in other religions.

If there is such an innate capacity within us for receiving messages from either divine or demonic sources, then we need to learn how to listen to God. New Age groups who teach 'channelling' are in effect opening themselves up to influences from any source without safeguards against possible demonic activities. Spiritualist mediums actively seek communion with the dead, and I have shown the negative results of such 'channelling' in my previous ch[...]
ter. Within the Christian Church it is necessary t[...]
prayers for such revelations specifically to *God*, a[...]

be subject to others giving confirmation of the divine source of any prophecies received (1 Corinthians 14:29).

One of the distinguishing features of John Wimber's ministry is that he tries to train ordinary Christians to be able to receive words of knowledge for themselves. As a result, they are often encouraged to listen to God and to speak out any words of knowledge which they might receive.

Some of these words of knowledge are not very detailed. They may be along the lines of, 'There is somebody here with a pain in the left shoulder,' or some similar common problem. These examples may be rather unconvincing. I suppose the disciples of Jesus must have had a similar problem, when suddenly Jesus turned around in a crowd and asked:

> 'Who touched my clothes?'
> 'You see the people crowding against you,' his disciples answered, 'and yet you can ask, "Who touched me?"'
> But Jesus kept looking around to see who had done it.
> (Mark 5:30–32, NIV)

John Gunstone has interpreted my findings as showing that 'very few Christians are gifted with a ministry of uttering authentic words of knowledge in open gatherings'.[10] Although this is true of a large group of Christians at any one point in time, there is also a process by which individuals may develop the gift in themselves. Most, perhaps all, of us have a *potential* for being open to these kinds of revelations. However, there are at least three major factors which can help or hinder their development.

Firstly, the type of church to which a person belongs has an important influence. If the church is open to receiving such revelations, there may be more opportunity for people to give them. Other kinds of churches may stifle any development of such gifts before they have a chance to be tried out.

Secondly, the frequency of such revelations seems to be

linked with a person's intimacy with God. One of those I interviewed about these matters told me that he is more likely to receive words of knowledge when he himself is walking closely with God. This also rings true in the experience of others, including myself. We can recognise that God does use imperfect and sinful people to fulfil his purposes – as none of us is perfect – but it seems significant also that John Wimber is now putting much more emphasis on the need among Christians for *holiness*.

Thirdly, giving out words of knowledge does involve the possibility of appearing to make a fool of oneself. Jesus seemed to be doing that when in a crowd he started to ask, 'Who touched me?' Those who follow him also need to be willing to speak out whatever God might be saying to them, silly as it might sound. For this reason, Wimber is sometimes quoted as saying that he spells 'faith' as 'r–i–s–k'.

Inner Healing

A second area of controversy about the extent to which New Age practices have 'infiltrated' the Christian Church concerns what is variously called 'inner healing', 'healing of the memories', 'emotional healing' or 'soul healing'. Essentially, this approach to healing is concerned with overcoming the effects of past hurts, because it is believed that traumas in the past, even in the womb, can affect attitudes and behaviour in the present. For example, it is thought that people who have lacked a human father figure or who have been abused by their fathers often have difficulty in relating to God as a heavenly 'Father'.

The assumptions and methods behind what is popularly known as 'inner healing' have been brought into question by Hunt and McMahon's book *The Seduction of Christianity*. More recently, the kinds of criticisms raised in *The Seduction of Christianity* have been developed in more detail by Don Matzat, in his book *Inner Healing: Deliverance or Deception?*[11] Matzat basically argues that the main

founders of 'inner healing', especially Agnes Sanford and
Morton Kelsey, took their ideas from secular psychology.
In particular, the ideas behind ministering to childhood
hurts buried in the subconscious are said to be taken from
Sigmund Freud's 'depth psychology'. Moreover, the
methods of 'visualising' Jesus in various scenes from the
past are said to have been borrowed from Carl Jung,
another major founder of modern psychology, who is said
to have become involved in some forms of the occult.

To a large extent, it is possible to accept this general
criticism of Agnes Sanford and Morton Kelsey even if one
might quibble with some of the details. However, influential practitioners of 'inner healing' are aware of some of
these difficulties and they warn against the uncritical use of
certain kinds of 'inner healing'. For example, Paul Yonggi
Cho, pastor of the world's largest church in Seoul, South
Korea, writes how some of the books recommended by
American ministers 'had almost made the subconscious
into an almighty god, and that is a great deception. The
subconscious has certain influence, but it is quite limited,
and cannot create like our Almighty God can.'[12]

In the same way, John Wimber writes,

I am using the term 'inner healing' sparingly . . . because
different authors use it to mean so many different things, many
of which I do not agree with. In many instances inner healing is
based on secular psychological views of how our personalities
are formed and influenced. But where these views contradict
the biblical teaching, they must be firmly rejected.[13]

In her book *How to Pray for Inner Healing*, Rita Bennett
writes that the 'two main ways to pray' are through 'reliving
the scene with Jesus' and through 'creative prayer'.[14] Both
involve what at first sight appear to be imaginary visualisations of hurtful scenes from a person's past. However, the
scene is then 're-enacted' in a positive way, with Jesus
present and ministering to, or simply being with, the person. From her writings, it would appear that all 'inner

healing' involves such visualisation, and these are the sources which are quoted by her critics.

Among many New Age groups and advocates of certain types of alternative medicine, one of the key *methods* used is the *visualisation* of the desired aim. This affects the subconscious and is supposed to help achieve results. Hunt and McMahon view the use of visualisation in 'inner healing' as a Christianised version of New Age techniques, which, they claim, derive ultimately from the kinds of shamanic religious practices traditionally found among various Siberian and Central Asian tribes.

However, although I came across many cases of 'inner healing' in my study of John Wimber's Harrogate conference, very few of them involved a person receiving a visual picture of Jesus of the kind described by Rita Bennett. Wimber in fact says that they do not encourage such visualisation. Instead, most instances of 'inner healing' were dealt with by *forgiveness*, *repentance*, *confession* and other widely recognised biblical principles, without recourse to 'visualisation'.[15]

Nevertheless, there *are* cases in which Jesus *does* appear to people and minister appropriately to their inner hurts. One of the most dramatic instances concerns 'Jill', a seventeen-year-old girl who had come to live with her pastor's family. The pastor's wife told me the following story:

. . . Her parents divorced when Jill was four years old. Her mother was anti-Christian and would have nothing in the house which was Christian. Jill became a Christian when she was ten and had to carry her Bible with her and sleep with it under her mattress or else it would be destroyed . . . Her mother's boyfriend subjected her to all forms of abuse – everything. Jill's sister who is two years younger had everything lavished upon her but Jill was totally deprived . . .

After she came to live here, she woke every night screaming with nightmares from what her mother's boyfriend had done to her. No man could go near, only I could . . .

[One night we] heard her rattling the door in her nightdress. We took her back to bed and as we were doing so we were

aware she was talking – in a very childish voice . . . She talked
as a four-year-old . . . It was the time of the divorce and
she relived it: horror and horror. ([Her mother's boyfriend]
sexually handled her, burned her, choked her – she was literally
going red in the face and not breathing: we couldn't believe what
we were experiencing.) She would even say what she had for
dinner – but at the end of the day said, 'My Jesus is coming. He's so
big.' It was so delightful. She gave a full description of how he was
dressed: 'Long, white and shiny, and a shiny thing round his waist.
Gold varnish on feet and hands, a pretty sticky-up thing on his
head – and his *eyes*, his *eyes* . . .' – four-year-old language. The
first one was 'Mummy's friend' but '*My* friend is big – my friend is
bigger than your friend. Mind your head, Jesus, don't bump your
head on the door.' Then he'd come and minister to her. He had
pockets on his robe: 'I wonder what he's got for me?' Cream to
soothe bruises or beating, plasters to put on. Something to eat –
she was starved as well. She would go through the motions – a big
strawberry milkshake . . .

There is no way in which I could attribute this girl's
experience to the influence of suggestion. In fact, Jill's
pastor and his wife recorded her later experiences and were
able to confirm the accuracy of her memories from her own
diaries. They took it in turns on successive nights to be
present in Jill's room when they began to hear her talking.
On two occasions, while Jill was being ministered to by
Jesus, they saw a mist or cloud filling part of the room. It
was so dense on the second occasion that it 'covered half a
chair, blotted out the dressing table and just a bit of the
mirror was poking out of the mist'. They later identified it
with the Shekhinah cloud of God's presence and glory
which is mentioned in the Bible (for example, Exodus 33:9;
2 Chronicles 5:13–14; Matthew 17:5).

One other detail further highlights the divine character
of Jill's visions. On one occasion, Jesus brought her a
knickerbocker glory ice-cream with a large strawberry at
the bottom. Later, when she went on holiday with her
pastor's family, they all decided to have knickerbocker

glories – Jill's first taste of a 'material' one. Hers alone turned out to have a large strawberry at its base![16]

Jill's experiences continued for a few months and were punctuated by a recurring vision of a house, the rooms of which symbolised various areas of her past life. As these were dealt with, the doors were shut on them. Finally, Jesus took her outside the front door and across the lawn to where her pastor and his wife were standing. He handed her over to them, indicating that her treatment was over. After this, her visions of Jesus ceased.

The extent of her healing is shown by the fact that she has now been accepted for training as a psychiatric nurse. During her interview for the course, she was asked how she felt about dealing with sexually-abused children. Jill replied that she could handle it because she had been through that experience herself. When asked if she needed counselling for it, she said that she did not need it and told the interviewers about her own experiences of healing. The fact that they recognised her healing and accepted her for training as a psychiatric nurse testifies to the effectiveness of what Jesus had done for her. Moreover, because of her own experiences, she now seems to have a special rapport with children who have been sexually abused; they instinctively seem to know they can trust Jill.

We have to ask, therefore, whether God can make use of *methods* at certain times which appear to parallel those of secular psychology. Essentially, we have to ask whether the one who created humanity and designed human psychology in the first place also knows the kinds of techniques which are most appropriate for healing it. Are these methods ones which God has made available because he knows that sometimes they might be necessary?

Confusion has arisen because of a failure to distinguish between *sources* and *methods*. The same confusion has arisen concerning words of knowledge and prophecies, because the *methods* (visions and strong 'intuitions') can be used both in spiritualism and in Christian contexts. In the same way, apparently similar *methods* for healing hurts from the past can be documented from both Christian and secular sources.

For physical healing it is clear that God makes use of a variety of *methods*, so why should the same not be true of emotional or psychological healing? The Gospels record that Jesus used many different *methods* for healing conditions which are all described as 'blindness' (though the causes in each case are not specified). On one occasion Jesus gave a word of command (Mark 10:52); on another occasion he spat in the blind man's eyes and then laid hands on them (Mark 8:23–25); and at another time he rebuked a demonic spirit causing the blindness (Matthew 12:22). On yet another occasion he spat on the ground and mixed his saliva with mud before applying it to the blind man's eyes and telling him to wash it off in the pool of Siloam (John 9:6–7).

It seems that Jesus may not have been the first to use spit in healing contexts but that he made use of an existing practice. In the same way, there are no scriptural precedents for the divine filling of dental cavities, but such miracles have been well-attested in recent decades from both North and South America.[17] If God can make use of *methods* which are widely used by dentists of all religious persuasions, or none, can he also make use of techniques for psychological or emotional healing which were humanly pioneered in other contexts?

Most biblical passages relating to forgiveness and Christian attitudes are addressed to groups rather than to individuals. Their focus is more on *preventing* the need for 'inner healing' than on giving directions on how to go about it. However, in actual practice the Holy Spirit appears to make use of a wide repertoire of *methods*, which in themselves might be neutral but can be used for either positive or negative ends.

There are more biblical examples of physical healing than of 'inner healing', but the two are often closely linked. Certainly from a medical point of view it is widely recognised that many types of physical illness can be helped by healing people's minds or attitudes.

Isaiah 61:1–2 (NIV) has been interpreted by Rita Bennett and others as referring to 'inner healing':

> The Spirit of the Sovereign Lord is on me, because the Lord has anointed me to preach good news to the poor. He has sent me to bind up the broken-hearted, to proclaim freedom for the captives and release from darkness for the prisoners, to proclaim the year of the Lord's favour and the day of vengeance of our God, to comfort all who mourn, and provide for those who grieve in Zion . . .

The fact that Jesus quoted part of this text in the synagogue at Nazareth and then announced, 'Today this scripture is fulfilled in your hearing' (Luke 4:21, NIV) is regarded as giving a further biblical precedent for 'inner healing'. Certainly Jesus had a noticeable compassion for the poor, and for widows and those who mourn (Matthew 5:3–5; Luke 7:11–17; Luke 18:1–8; Luke 21:1–4). He also spoke of being let off one's debts as an image of having one's sins forgiven (Matthew 6:12; 18:21–35); this ties in with the idea that Isaiah 61:1–2 is referring to a year when all debts will be cancelled, according to the law of Moses (Leviticus 25:8–55; Deuteronomy 15:1–11). Jesus himself paid those debts for us, that our sins might be forgiven: in this sense, his whole ministry was concerned with 'inner healing'.

Two clear examples in which Jesus focused first on what we would now call 'inner healing' before he healed physically can be found in Luke 5:17–26 and John 5:1–15. In Luke 5:20 (NIV), the first words that Jesus spoke to a paralytic were, 'Friend, your sins are forgiven.' He did not heal the man's physical condition immediately. To a man who had a very similar condition, who was unable to walk for some reason, Jesus first asked, 'Do you want to get well?' (John 5:6, NIV). His concern was first of all with the person's *will* and *attitude*. Later, Jesus told this man, 'Stop sinning or something worse may happen to you' (John

5:14). David Pytches comments: 'In this case – but by no means always (John 9:3) – the man's infirmity had come through some sin. To return to that sin was to open up the door for the infirmity to return in a worse form.'[18]

'Inner healing' was also important in the case of the woman described in Luke 8:43–48 who suffered from menhorragia, persistent bleeding through her vagina. According to the Mosaic law:

> When a woman has a discharge of blood for many days at a time other than her monthly period or has a discharge that continues beyond her period, she will be unclean as long as she has the discharge, just as in the days of her period. Any bed she lies on while her discharge continues will be unclean, as is her bed during her monthly period, and anything she sits on will be unclean, as during her period. Whoever touches them will be unclean; he must wash his clothes and bathe with water, and he will be unclean till evening.
>
> (Leviticus 15:25–27, NIV)

The woman described in Luke 8:43–48 had been in this condition for *twelve years*. Once we understand these social implications of her condition, we can recognise that it was not enough for her to receive her physical healing anonymously. Her healing had to be made public knowledge, embarrassing as that might be. Therefore the way in which Jesus drew attention to her healing, and her public acknowledgments of her former condition and also of her healing, were very important elements in her own 'inner healing' and in her restoration to normal social life.[19]

More specifically in terms of 'healing of the memories', there is the incident recorded in John 21:15–19 (NIV) where Jesus asks Peter three times, 'Do you love me?' Commentators rightly compare this with Peter's earlier denials that he was a disciple of Jesus, although Jesus did not refer directly to those earlier incidents. Instead, he called forth a reaffirmation of Peter's love and then commissioned Peter afresh. The past was no longer a barrier to their relationship and Peter could go on to lead the Church in the power of the Holy Spirit.

Predictive Prophecy

The 'charismatic movement' in this century has tended to progress from one emphasis to another, each one being controversial at first but then gradually becoming more widely accepted. In the past, the focus has been more upon speaking in tongues and styles of worship. More recently, there has been 'renewal' and debate focused upon 'words of knowledge'. Now, a new emphasis on predictive prophecy has become more prominent.

Some Christians are wary of predictive prophecy because it reminds them too much of the claims of psychics like Edgar Cayce or the attempts by astrologers to predict future events on the basis of planetary movements. The very term 'New Age' is itself based upon astrological assumptions about the 'Age of Aquarius'.

In John Wimber's Vineyard movement this new focus on predictive prophecy arose through John's contact with an American prophet named Paul Cain. Towards the end of 1988, when Paul Cain went to visit John Wimber in southern California, Cain predicted in advance that on the day he arrived in California there would be a 'sign in the ground'. This sign would confirm that his message was truly from God. That very morning, at 3:38, there was a 'shaking'-type earthquake in southern California, which left no casualties. Even though earthquakes do occur in California, statistically the odds against accurately predicting the date of one are still very high. Moreover, after Paul Cain arrived he delivered to John Wimber a highly specific message (relating to recent sins among some of Wimber's colleagues) which was also focused around the promise in Jeremiah 33:8. Not only the date of the earthquake but also its very *timing* confirmed what Paul Cain had to say.[20]

In an example like this, the use of predictive prophecy

often has a *moral* dimension. The importance of such fulfilled prophecy lies not so much in its confirmed accuracy, important as that is, but rather in its *confirmation* of the truth of the prophet's message. Biblical prophets spoke God's words to their generation but sometimes provided proof of their authority through the signs which accompanied their messages. Examples include the fire which fell from heaven on Elijah's sacrifice, as a sign that it was offered to the true God (1 Kings 18:22–39), and the shadow which went back up the steps as a sign to Hezekiah (2 Kings 20:2–11; Isaiah 38:2–8).

Another American prophet is Bob Jones, who belongs to a fellowship in Kansas City pastored by Mike Bickle. In April 1983 God told Bickle to call God's people in the city together, to fast and pray for twenty-one days. On the following day his directions were independently confirmed by Bob Jones, who had received the same instructions from an angel. Once the fasting and prayer had been arranged, it was accompanied on the first night by the appearance of a comet unpredicted by scientists but predicted by Bob Jones. Then on the last day of the fast Bob Jones proclaimed: '. . . In this city everything will be withheld. For three months there will be a drought. That's the sign! God has spoken! The drought for three months is because they have rejected the call to fast – they have mocked God. But for three months there will be no rain – not till August 23rd.' This prediction was fulfilled precisely: there was no rain at all for the next three months, until at 6:00 pm on 23rd August 1983 the drought was broken by a great downpour of rain.[21]

Accounts like this, though reminiscent of Elijah's prediction of a drought in the reign of Ahab (1 Kings 17:1–18:45), nevertheless raise questions in the minds of many people. What is strange and unfamiliar can often appear threatening. They feel uncomfortable with the concept of a God who brings drought or earthquake today. Although they recognise that such events did occur in the Old Testament, they prefer the New Testament emphasis that God is love, with the implication that he would not do these kinds of things today.

In fact, this 'prophetic' kind of Christianity, which sees the hand of God in at least some earthquakes and droughts today, is far more biblical than many of us would like to admit. Even in the New Testament there are instances of sickness and death coming as divine judgment on individuals who deliberately sin (Acts 5:1–11; 13:9–12; 1 Corinthians 11:29–30). The prophet Agabus accurately predicted a severe famine (Acts 11:28–30). Although this is not stated explicitly to be an instance of divine judgment, God nevertheless warned his people so that they could prepare for it and supply the needs of the poor. (The same was true of the famine in Egypt at the time of Joseph, described in Genesis 41–47, except that the warning was given to the whole nation through Joseph's interpretation of Pharaoh's dream.)

Elsewhere in the New Testament there are many more general predictions about famines, earthquakes and other disasters which would be signs of the end of the age (for example, Matthew 24, Mark 13 or Luke 21:5–36, and most of the book of Revelation). In Revelation (especially chapters 6, 8, 9, 15 and 16) many of these disasters are depicted as being due to divine judgment. To at least some extent, these judgments might occur simply through God's *withdrawal* of his protection (Romans 1:18–32; 2 Thessalonians 2:7–12).

In the Bible there are a number of apparently *immutable* predictive prophecies, such as the seven years of plenty followed by seven of famine in ancient Egypt (Genesis 41) and the succession of human empires (Babylonian, Medo-Persian, Greek and Roman) leading up to God's establishment of 'a kingdom that will never be destroyed' (Daniel 2). The 'God in heaven who reveals mysteries' (Daniel 2:28) did reveal certain truths about the future to Gentile monarchs (Pharaoh and Nebuchadnezzar) but the *interpretation* of these dreams came through Joseph and Daniel. The *partial* revelation given to these Gentiles was made more complete through those who had a greater revelation from God. In the same way, the Magi were receptive to divine revelations through dreams (Matthew 2:12) and the star which they followed was merely the sign which led them to Jesus.

By contrast, many other predictive prophecies in the Bible are *conditional* upon the people's repentance or lack of it. Unfortunately, the people of Israel did not usually repent and so they suffered exile and other disasters which had been predicted, whereas the people of Ninevah did repent on hearing Jonah's message and were spared.

Similarly, some revelations given today are conditional upon repentance. Others, however, are *warnings* prompting us to action. They can be compared with God's warnings to the wise men that they should return by another route and to Joseph that he should flee with his family to Egypt (Matthew 2:13). In the same way, a woman I used to know in Leeds was prompted by a dream to pray for Mrs Thatcher's protection shortly before an attempt was made to take her life by a bomb planted at a hotel in Brighton.

Although these are some of the more dramatic cases of predictive prophecy, it might be that many more prophets are around in our churches whose ministries are not recognised so clearly by the wider Church. For example, I recently met in Cambridge a Christian named Peter Vernan, who claimed that in 1982 God had shown him that he was handing the people of Britain over to their false gods. As a result of this, there would be various kinds of disasters, including incidents in which people would die *en masse* in football stadia. He said that more recently he saw in advance a stock market collapse and the sudden political changes in Eastern Europe.

The various factors which help or hinder the recognition of such prophetic giftings are similar to those already discussed for words of knowledge. These include a church environment which is open to such revelations and is willing to test them out, a close walk with God on the part of the prophet and a willingness to risk telling others about those revelations which have been received.

Sometimes both words of knowledge and prophetic revelations come from simply asking the right questions and waiting on God for the answers. St Paul prayed for the Philippian church, that their love may 'abound more and more in *knowledge and depth of insight*' (Philippians 1:9, my italics). A similar connection between *prayer* and *insight* can be seen in the experience of Daniel. He sought God, pleading with him 'in prayer and petition, in fasting, and in sackcloth and ashes' (Daniel 9:3). As a result, Gabriel came to give him *'insight and understanding'* (Daniel 9:22, my italics). The specific revelations to Paul Cain and Bob Jones have often been via angels but these are men who also spend long hours alone with God in prayer.

These various 'signs' are above all *pointers* to God and *confirmations* of his messages. They are not mere intellectual curiosities. The signs force us also to face up to the implications for our own lives. Often this process leads to repentance and a renewed commitment to the Lord, which is the fruit that God desires.

10

Comparing Christianity and New Age

The Christian response to New Age must not simply be in
words – however important, straightforward and clear
these words might be – but in the hard, human evidence of
lives transformed and irradiated by the power and peace of
God. The sad yet gifted Oscar Wilde showed some perception when he said, 'In the English church a man succeeds
not through his capacity for belief, but through his capacity
for disbelief. Ours is the only church where the sceptic
stands at the altar, and where St Thomas is regarded as the
ideal apostle.' The Church has paid a heavy price for her
uncertainty, her compromise and her refusal to recapture
the beating heart of New Testament Christianity. New Age
is only one of the manifestations of the desire to fill the
vacuum which can only be satisfactorily filled by God in
Jesus Christ reconciling the world to himself.

I was preparing to preach at the closing communion
service of a great Christian festival in the west of Scotland
when it seemed that God spoke directly into my heart
giving me a vision for the Church and enabling me to
understand what was in God's heart. It was the vision of a
Church which would stop shooting itself in the foot by its
internal wranglings and denominational suspicions and
would instead unite behind the cross of Christ to proclaim
the transforming Gospel in the power of the Holy Spirit. It
was the vision of a Church demonstrating God's power as
well as declaring God's word, so that God could be seen as
well as heard – embracing the gifts of the Holy Spirit as well
as the fruit of the Holy Spirit so that our nation would see

what Jesus can do as well as what Jesus is like. It was the vision of a Church which takes young people seriously and by the grace of God releases them to be the Church of today rather than the Church of tomorrow – free from the restrictions, reservations and hesitancies which my generation has grown up with. It was the vision of the Church becoming what God always intended it to be – the new body of Christ on earth – providing salt to challenge social corruption and injustice and fertiliser to promote growth in righteousness, goodness and truth; at the same time providing light to break into the darkness of deception, hypocrisy and despair. It was the vision of the Church longing after holiness of life and transparency of character so that what we say is never contradicted by what we are.

Such was my vision and dream on that early spring morning. Such is my conviction if we are ever going to have an honourable and real response to the New Age.

The course of all human history was changed nearly 2,000 years ago when a Man died on a Cross . . . Calvary is finished, its powerful current inevitably touching every human life and death. Yet, too many still fail to feel its pulsating power. Jesus Christ not only represents life at its richest, He is life in all its vitality and abundance. Yet, more and more spiritually hungry Americans are turning, not to Christianity for healing and fulfilment, but to Eastern mysticism – the New Age philosophy, which has snaked its way into the boardrooms of corporate America and even into high levels of our nation's government.

So wrote Jack Hayford, the Senior Pastor of 'The Church on the Way', Van Nuys, California.[1]

However, as in the United States so in the United Kingdom, the response we must make is not to bemoan the emergence of New Age and the like but to call the Church away from its obsessional worship of the relics of its past and redirect its exclusive focus on the thrilling prophecies about the future. Only then can it begin to minister out of the full richness and power of God's resources to a spiritually hungry world today.

Common Ground between New Age and Christianity

Before we look at the fundamental conflicts between New Age and Christianity it would be well to see that there is a *convergence* between the two. The strength and subtlety of New Age largely lies in that it capitalises on two areas which are fundamental to the whole Christian message.

1. The spiritual is important

Sir Thomas Browne once gave man an unusual title; he called him 'the great amphibian'. He was attempting to convey the reality that man really is a creature of two worlds. He is at home in the visible, tangible world of space and time, but there are deep and insatiable longings within him for the unseen world which will forever be breaking into his consciousness. A padre in World War I who became known as Woodbine Willie (his real name was J. Studdart Kennedy) put this into verse:

> I'm a man, and a man's a mixture,
> Right down from his very birth.
> For part of him comes from heaven
> And part of him comes from earth.

It is not possible to explain man purely in terms of this world. Chemical analysis shows that the average man contains enough fat to make seven bars of soap; enough iron to make a medium-sized nail; enough sugar to fill a sugar-sifter; enough lime to whitewash a hen-house; enough potassium to explode a toy cannon; enough magnesium for a dose of magnesia; enough phosphorus to make tips for 2,200 matches; and a very little sulphur. You could buy the whole lot for a few pounds. However, you could take your few pounds and buy these chemicals and proceed to attempt to bring them all together – but the result would never be a man.

One of the curious facts which used to fascinate the

ancient Greeks was that a living body and the dead body of the same person would weigh exactly the same – yet something had gone, and that something was the something which makes the body into a living human being, a person. Man is unquestionably a creature of two worlds. Every now and then every one of us becomes aware of that other world of which he also forms a part.

The theologians talk of what they call the *numinous* – that which cannot be determined nor analysed by the five senses of hearing, sight, smell, taste or touch but is nevertheless real in human experience. One theologian speaks of 'the wholly other' in life that invades every life at some time. During World War II a story used to be told of an army sergeant who one evening declared that he was an uncompromising atheist and that he had no use whatever for any belief in God. The very next day he and some of his men were caught unexpectedly in a dive-bombing raid. Having no cover, they had no alternative but desperately to scrabble out a fox-hole in the earth and wait. As the planes came over in repeated waves, each one unloading its explosive cargo all around the group, the men were astonished to hear the sergeant crying out to God in prayer unashamedly above the noise. One of them said: 'I thought you were an atheist!' 'Son', replied the sergeant, 'there are no atheists in fox-holes.'[2] Christian prayer may be distinctive but prayer is instinctive. That is why even the agnostic was compelled to pray reluctantly: 'O God, if there is a God, save my soul, if I have a soul!'[3]

Man is more than a programmed animal or a finely-tuned machine. He has spiritual capacities that not only need to be recognised but also need to be exercised. The man who says, 'I am not religious,' is neither being honest with himself nor with those to whom he is protesting. Man's choice does not lie in whether he will be religious or not; man's choice lies in what his religion is going to be. New Age will stress the unlimited potential of self-realised human gods, whereas Christians will stress the immeasurable potential of human beings made in the image of God –

not only made by God but also made for God. Christians will stress that man by himself is unable to know that warm, intimate relationship with God for which he was created, so God has taken the initiative and sent his Son into the world to be man's redeemer. So, cleansed and redeemed by the sacrificial death of Christ on the cross, man is able to enter into living fellowship with the God for whom he was created. He now faces the possibility of living on earth the life for which he was intended in the power of the Holy Spirit.

Both New Age and Christianity recognise in all of this that spiritual reality must be perceived and satisfied – although they differ radically in the means they suggest towards achieving this.

2. *A sense of purpose and meaning to life is important*

In the year AD 627 Edwin, King of Northumbria, pressed hard by the missionary Paulinus, was in two minds over whether to accept Christianity or not. He called a council of his wise men and asked them what they thought of this new faith. Coifi, the head of the heathen priests, spoke in cynical vein. In the silence which followed, one of the warriors addressed the company in the following now-famous words:

The present life of men upon earth, O King, seems to me in comparison with that land which is unknown to us, like to the swift flight of a sparrow through that house wherein you sit at supper in winter, with your ealdormen and thegns, while the fire blazes in the midst and the hall is warmed, but the winter storms of rain or snow are raging abroad. The sparrow flying in at one door and immediately out at another whilst he is within is safe from the wintry tempest, but after a short space of fair weather he immediately vanishes out of your sight, passing from winter into winter again, so this life of man appears for a little while, but of what is to follow or what went before, we know nothing at all. If therefore this new doctrine tells us something more certain, it seems justly to deserve to be followed.[4]

This persuaded Edwin to accept the Christian faith – a decision that had considerable historical significance in the development of our nation. What the warrior had done was to highlight man's inborn sense of insecurity in a world full of doubt and uncertainty. Because man stands facing dark, uncharted regions that lie beyond his 'ken', he is not so ready to dismiss answers which claim to cast a measure of light upon the ultimate mystery.

As in the seventh century, so in the twentieth – although man may now have his space-probes, his ability to fly easily at twice the speed of sound, his medical skill to transplant heart and lungs, his satellite communications – he is no more at home in this world than those Anglo-Saxon thanes were in theirs, shivering in the winter cold of ancient Northumbria. W. H. Auden speaks of this age as being the age of anxiety. 'Mankind,' says Lewis Mumford, 'is afloat on a frail life raft. Religion understands the mysteries of the deep and the storms that come up on the night.'[5] There is a chronic sense of uncertainty, anxiety and bewilderment which is characteristic of the human race. Man is constantly searching for purpose and meaning so that he will have understanding of his life.

Paul Tillich the theologian, in his book *The Courage to Be*, draws a distinction between what he calls pathological and existential anxiety. The pathological victim needs the help of a skilled psychiatrist, whereas someone suffering the normal kinds of anxiety, insecurity and uncertainty about the ultimate purpose of life, must look for help not in the direction of medicine but of religion – that is, not in the direction of the material but in the direction of the spiritual. According to Tillich there are three dominant elements in this universal and normal form of anxiety – no matter how well they may be covered up within our culture. First, he says, there is a deep ineradicable sense of guilt in human nature to which all the great literature of the world bears witness. This results in a feeling of foreboding and suppressed apprehension. Second, there is the fear of death. We may not visit the cemetery as often as previous generations but deep within us there is a lurking fear that one day all our accomplishments and potentialities will perish in an awesome final extinction. In a previous generation the taboo subject of polite conversation was sex, but in this generation sex is freely talked of but death is spurned. What we hesitate to speak of we often fear. Third, there is a sense of blank meaninglessness, Tillich says. Even the professional sceptics who have long since said goodbye to the God of orthodoxy, have spent strenuous years trying to discern some cosmic plan or intelligence behind the flux and flow of phenomena. No one can ever be really happy in the belief that life is at the mercy of blind chance. From this the soul of man recoils in horror.[6]

The discovery of purpose and meaning to life are goals much sought after – albeit unconsciously – by man. The New Age steps on to this platform by seeing man as part of a move towards a new and perfect world. This will be achieved by a totally new way of thinking (a 'paradigm shift'). The mind train will no longer be analytical, rational, objective, using linear thought (where every effect must have a cause) but instead have an intuitional, holistic approach, subject to feelings and experience (e.g. 'If it feels right, it is right') which reconciles all opposites. There will be no ethical values: good and evil are merely different. God is all and all is God. In this way, New Age responds to the persistent craving in the soul of man for meaning and purpose.

The Christian responds by declaring that the ultimate meaning of life lies in God himself and not in man. He created us because he is love. Before the earth, the sun, moon and stars, was God. The fact is that it is not just that he loves us (although that is true!) but he is love. That simple statement is not to be found in any other religion. To say that God is love is to affirm that God must be more than one person. God must be relationships. One person by himself cannot *be* love! Fundamental to Christian belief is that from the beginning God has always been more than one person. He is Father, Son and Holy Spirit. However little we may be able to grasp this with our minds we know that the three persons in the Godhead (the Trinity) are so deeply involved with one another that in our humanity we can hardly tell the difference between them. For example, when we talk to the Father it is like talking to the Son; and when we respond to the Spirit it is like responding to the Father and when we trust the Son it is like trusting the Spirit.

It is here then that the ultimate meaning and purpose of life lies: God, because he is love, wanted a bigger family. It is the nature of true love that it wants to share itself with more and more. This is the ultimate reason for parents having children; the love which they share with one another wants to extend its ability to share, and so a new life is created in order that this can happen. God's intention and desire is to have a family so that the deep, tender, strong love that he is in himself can be shared and enjoyed in a much wider circle. So man was created in order that he could receive God's love and then voluntarily respond to it. In God's heart was not only the desire to share his love with man, but a desire that relationships within the family would be the same as those God enjoyed – and enjoys – within himself.

Although completely different from New Age, Christianity finds the 'existential vacuum' or meaninglessness of life unacceptable too, and challenges it with a God revealed in Jesus Christ who not only loves but is himself love.

The Differences Between New Age and Christianity

Although both New Age and Christianity affirm the reality and importance of the spiritual, and declare that life has an ultimate meaning and a definite purpose, they are also widely divergent. There can be – and there must be – no confusion between the two. The foregoing chapters will have already demonstrated this, even to those, with a minimal concept of the Christian faith. However, I

want now to list some of the many *differences* between
Christianity and New Age.

1. Self versus others

Elsewhere in this book it is amply demonstrated that New
Age lays a great emphasis on self-fulfilment and the discovery of oneself. The focus is on man and his need.
Christianity at its heart is God-centred! In a moving cry
from the heart, especially bearing in mind his very
considerable human benefits and richness, the apostle Paul
declared:

> . . . I reckon everything as complete loss for the sake of what is
> so much more valuable, the knowledge of Christ Jesus my
> Lord. For his sake I have thrown everything away; I consider it
> all as mere refuse, so that I may gain Christ and be completely
> united with him.
>
> (Philippians 3:8–9, GNB)

So it was that that amazing young man, C. T. Studd,
nurtured in the lap of comfort, educated at Eton and
Cambridge, the hero of the British sport-loving public,
whose Cambridge career had been described as 'one long
blaze of cricketing glory', created a stir in the secular world
of his youth by renouncing wealth and position to follow
Christ. He was captain of the Eton XI in 1879, and of
Cambridge University in 1883, being accorded in that same
year 'the premier position as an all-round cricketer for the
second year in succession'.[7]

The illness of his brother brought him face to face with
reality and with the transitory nature of wealth and fame.
He obeyed the divine command to another as God's direction for him: '. . . sell all you have and give the money to
the poor, and you will have riches in heaven; then come and
follow me' (Mark 10:21, GNB). He had inherited a part of
his father's fortune when he was twenty-five, and in one
memorable day, 13th January 1887, he disposed of all of it

to people and causes involved in fulfilling the will of God in the world. From then on his life was dedicated to the will and service of God and his fellow men. His life-story is an epic of faith and courage against great odds which was based on his conclusion: 'If Jesus Christ be God, and died for me; there is no sacrifice too great for me to make for Him.'[8]

The heart-cry of Christianity is not self-fulfilment but self-denial, not for its own sake but in order to bless God and benefit mankind. Jesus exemplified this in his own life, and so it must be for all who would follow him.

2. Subjective experience or reality?

New Age is based on subjective personal experience (if it feels right then it is right). The Christian faith is not based on philosophy or mysticism but on objective, factual, observable, historical reality. The Bible is not a book of ideas but a book of fact. Jesus is a real, historical figure. Christianity is an historical religion.

'I know men,' said Napoleon Bonaparte, 'and I tell you that Jesus Christ is no mere man. Between him and every other person in the world there is no possible term of comparison. Alexander, Caesar, Charlemagne and I have founded empires. But on what did we rest the creations of our genius? Upon force. Jesus Christ founded His empire on love; and at this hour millions of men would die for Him.'[9] In the same way Wilbur Smith writes about the historical comparison between Jesus and other great figures on the stage of history: 'The latest edition of the *Encyclopedia Britannica* gives twenty thousand words to this person Jesus, and does not even hint that He did not exist – more words, by the way, than are given to Aristotle, Alexander, Cicero, Julius Caesar, or Napoleon Bonaparte.'[10]

On the basis of such a reality, obedience to the revealed and known will of God is the Christian's reason for being. Writing to Christians who were under the pressure of great persecution from the civil authorities Peter says, 'You were chosen according to the purpose of God the Father and were made a holy people by his Spirit, to obey Jesus Christ and be purified by his blood' (1 Peter 1:2, GNB).

3. God is in all – or is he?

New Age in its desire for unity and harmony sees man as becoming one with nature and the cosmos. Inevitably it has expressed concern for conservation and a deep interest in ecology. As it develops this strand in its thinking it concludes that nature is God. Christianity strongly refutes this pantheistic understanding of God and is committed to the view that since God is the creator he is separate from that which he has created. Pantheism identifies the universe with God and so shuts him up in his own world. Christianity perceives God to be both involved in the world, and yet above and beyond the world. To put it in technical language, Christianity declares that God is at one and the same time both immanent and transcendent: he is at once in the world and beyond the world; at one and the same time sharing life and directing life. 'There is no one like the Lord our God. He lives in the heights above,' says the Psalmist, 'but He bends down to see the heavens and the earth' (Psalm 113:5–6, GNB).

4. A soul-less force – or a person?

To the New Ager, God is a 'soul-less force'; he is impersonal, remote, removed. To the Christian, God is a person. He has no body – and yet Christians believe that God has a heart and a mind and a will. The Bible speaks of his arms being underneath us; his ears being open to us; his hand being upon us. God has no birthdays – he is from everlasting to everlasting, eternal – and yet Christians believe that he was prepared to leave heaven and live among us.

A Christian man used to visit the very poorest part of the city of Cardiff. He would climb the steps of the grey, unyielding tenement buildings and talk to people about the love of God. One day, standing outside the door of a house he had just visited, he overheard one of the people inside say to another: 'It's all very well for him to come and talk about the love of God, but he doesn't live here. He lives in a nice house on the other side of Cardiff.'

The Christian sold his house and went to live in that tenement. So God 'laid aside His majesty; gave up everything for me; suffered at the hands of those He had created. He took all my sin and shame when He died and rose again.'[11] God came from glory and was born in a dirty, exposed stable – where you and I would never choose to have our babies born. This, Christians believe.

We are made to resemble him (Genesis 1:26) and Jesus taught us to call him Father.

5. *Great moral teacher – or Son of God?*

Jesus is considered to be a master of wisdom in New Age thinking – and this he undoubtedly is. Sholem Ash, a Jew, speaks of Jesus in this way:

> Jesus Christ is the outstanding personality of all time . . . No other teacher – Jewish, Christian, Buddhist, Mohammedan – is *still* a teacher whose teaching is such a guidepost for the world we live in. Other teachers may have something basic for an Oriental, an Arab, or an Occidental; but every act and word of Jesus has value for all of us. He became the Light of the World. Why shouldn't I, a Jew, be proud of that.[12]

However, the Christian categorically declares him also to be God – a claim indicated in the Bible (e.g. Philippians 2:6–11) C. S. Lewis wrote:

> I am trying here to prevent anyone saying the really foolish thing that people often say about Him: 'I'm ready to accept Jesus as a great moral teacher, but I don't accept His claim to be God.' That is the one thing we must not say. A man who was merely a man and said the sort of things Jesus said would not be

a great moral teacher. He would either be a lunatic – on a level with the man who says he is a poached egg – or else He would be the Devil of Hell. You must make your choice. Either this man was, and is, the Son of God; or else a madman or something worse.[13]

6. What moral attributes does God have?

To New Agers God is all and is in all. On the face of it, that is a lavish and acceptable claim. However, when it is clinically broken down it means that God can be bad as well as good. But to Christians this is absurd for God is un-equivocally good. 'How good you are – how kind!' says the Psalmist. 'Teach me your commands' (Psalm 119:68, GNB).

A theme of Shakespeare's *Measure for Measure* is the dilemma of imperfect people trying to apply the laws of perfect morality. An apparently upright judge distorts justice under the impact of a sudden temptation to lust. He then goes on to deny clemency to a young man guilty of the very sin he himself is contemplating. This raises all sorts of questions, and if answers could be given they would be summed up in these words:

> They say best men are moulded out of faults,
> And for the most become much more the better
> For being a little bad.[14]

Simply stated – we live in an imperfect world and we must learn to live with imperfections. This is why many prefer to believe in the God they would like rather than the God who has revealed himself in the Bible – as perfect.

7. Do all roads lead to God?

In New Age there is a clear syncretism: all roads lead to God. As the world becomes more like a global village there has been a corresponding and profound awareness of other religions impinging upon our lives. Other faiths are no longer academically considered in books but actually confronted in everyday life. So inter-faith theology has emerged and become commonplace. What you believe is valid and effective for you because you believe it. Intolerance has become frowned upon and rejected while tolerance has an appeal of sophistication and normality.

However, for the Christian there is a uniqueness and absolute intolerance so far as Jesus is concerned. He is not one among many – he is the only way to God. The clearest statement of this in the New Testament is in Acts 4:12 – 'Salvation is to be found through him alone; in all the world there is no one else whom God has given who can save us.' Someone once said, 'It's not the parts of the Bible I don't understand which worry me; it's the parts of the Bible I do understand.' Not only does the Bible give what no other religion gives – forgiveness – but Christianity cannot be fitted into any other religion. There is only one way to God and that is by Jesus (see also Isaiah 46:9; John 14:6).

8. Can man escape his lower instincts?

It is hard in the twentieth century to continue to believe that human beings are getting better, especially since it has been called the Century of Blood. In no other century has there been more carnage through war – or more wars for that matter. Yet for New Agers there is the astonishing commitment to the idea of evolution in human beings as the plan and purpose behind the universe. This theory rests on the assumption that what the theologians call sin is merely a survival of our animal heritage. It is the result of physical passions and vital impulses, but once man acquires a civilised veneer the downward drag of heredity will gradually disappear.

The fallacy at the heart of this view is belief that sin is essentially animal, not human. Dostoevsky, in his novel *The Brothers Karamazov*, tears this myth to shreds. He has one of his characters say:

A Bulgarian I met lately in Moscow told me of the crime committed by Turks and Caucasians in Bulgaria through fear of the general rising of the Slavs – they burn villages, outrage women and children; they nail children by the ear to the fences, leave them there till the morning and in the morning they hang them – all sorts of things you can't imagine. People talk sometimes of bestial cruelty, but that's a grave injustice and insult to the beasts. A beast can never be as cruel as a man, as artistically cruel. The tiger only tears and gnaws – that is all he can do, but he would never think of nailing people by the ear even were he able to do it.[15]

The logic is unanswerable: sin by its very nature is distinctively human. The key to understanding history is salvation by the mercy and grace of God (Isaiah 51:6). It is salvation, not evolution, to which the Christian is committed. But for the New Ager there is little recognition of man's sinfulness and the consequent need for salvation. The New Ager lays a great emphasis on man's higher divine nature and his inherent potential for self-redemption. Christians historically have never doubted that man is a fallen creature and that his nature is sinful (Romans 3:23).

New Age philosophy urges us to accept ourselves as we are whereas the Christian Gospel urges us to repent of our sin and be reconciled to a holy and righteous God through his Son Jesus. This alone brings life.

9. Is Christ's death meaningful?

As a result of the above, New Agers regard the death of Christ as insignificant and irrelevant. Christians regard the cross of Christ as central to salvation and to the establishment of the kingdom of God: 'Through the Son, then, God decided to bring the whole universe back to himself. God made peace through his Son's death on the cross and so brought back to himself all things, both on earth and in heaven' (Colossians 1:20, GNB). So the cross becomes the accepted symbol of the Christian faith. Between one third and one half of the Gospels is devoted to the passion and death of Jesus Christ who obviously lived as though his death was the most important feature of his life. Significantly, the Apostles' Creed goes straight from the birth of Christ to his death with no reference to his mighty ministry and his amazing miracles. The central act of Christianity is the Communion service; it is there that Jesus chose to be remembered – in his death. The cross was the means God chose to separate the sinner from his sin – rescuing one and destroying the other. So Jesus was made sin that we might be made righteous. So it was that the devil was vanquished; the world was reconciled to God; God's holiness was honoured; the Law was fully satisfied; and the sinner's guilt was taken away.

10. Can man reach God?

Self-effort and doing good works loom large in New Age: man has to struggle towards God. The initiative and responsibility is on man's side. The unique characteristic of Christianity is that God has come to us. In all the great religions of the world the emphasis is on man's search for God. In Christianity alone the emphasis is on God's search for man. 'For it is by God's grace that you have been saved through faith. It is not the result of your own efforts,' cries the Apostle Paul, 'but God's gift, so that no one can boast about it' (Ephesians 2:8–9, GNB). We become Christians with our ears not with our hands.

Christians do not do good things in order to get to heaven, for they have already won acceptance; they do good things because they are already going there, having been accepted because of what Christ has done on the cross. At Bethlehem Jesus brought God to man; at Calvary Jesus brought man to God – but it is always Jesus and not 'me'.

11. The origin and process of spiritual growth

New Age affirms that spiritual growth will come through occult knowledge. For the Christian, however, the source

of all spiritual growth will be a real relationship with God,
made possible by what Jesus has done on the cross, and
made actual through the ministry of the Holy Spirit.

> I . . . ask the God of our Lord Jesus Christ, the glorious
> Father, to give you the Spirit, who will make you wise and
> reveal God to you, so that you will know him. I ask that your
> minds may be opened to see his light, so that you will know
> what is the hope to which he has called you, how rich are the
> wonderful blessings he promises his people.
>
> (Ephesians 1:17, 18, GNB)

God never intended that we should remain weak, immature and vulnerable but instead that we should grow and
develop and become strong. Again, it is the initiative of
God that makes this possible through his Son and by his
Spirit. This does not remove personal responsibility, but
does require personal co-operation.

12. Are emotions and experiences the basis for faith?

New Age lays a great emphasis on the reaction and
response of our feelings: our emotional reality has a very
high profile, and the subjective dominates the objective.
Experience-based, untheological Christianity has encouraged the 'feelings are authoritative' mode of New Age.
Christianity is based on biblical revelation: it is a revealed
religion and has its roots in history where it is verifiable.
This releases Christianity not only from authentication by
feelings but also from fiction and fantasy. The hallmark of
Christianity is historical fact.

Christianity respects and acknowledges human emotion
as an important part of human nature just as it does the
human mind. But it also insists that you can touch a man's
mind and his heart and yet not have got through to the real
person: the will is the central citadel of the human personality. Feelings may accompany or follow activity which is
founded on fact – but they are not the decisive element.

Feelings will vary according to a whole range of factors, but the facts of the matter remain constant. This alone will give constancy and stability to faith.

13. *Meditation – focusing on what?*

Meditation is allied to diet, posture, and the time of the year for cleansing the mind, in New Age. For the Christian, meditation will always be on the word of God assisted by the Holy Spirit and a right attitude of heart. 'Help me to understand your laws,' pleads the Psalmist, 'and I will meditate on your wonderful teachings' (Psalm 119:27, GNB).

To clear the mind and have it blank is to be open to the intrusion of influences which are not of God. This is simply another instance of Christianity insisting on objective fact rather than subjective feeling. The safeguard for real and healthy meditation is the revealed heart of God in his Word.

14. *The paranormal – to the glory of man or of God?*

New Agers are fascinated by the paranormal, which leads all too often to a self-centred glorification of man. For Christians the supernatural is a reality, for God has called us to live a naturally supernatural life; however, this always glorifies God. A miracle is a *natural* event in that it takes place within the context of the natural, normal world with which we are so familiar. A miracle is also an *unnatural* event in that it takes a course or a direction which would not be the normal, natural and expected course for it to take. A miracle is, in addition, a *supernatural* event in that it has a cause or origin which is outside the sphere of nature: it comes from God himself. So Christians have the expectancy of moving constantly in this supernatural dimension – but it is the dimension of the spiritual rather than the sensational. Such supernatural phenomena will always glorify God and not man.

When Jesus healed a man who had to be lowered to him

through the roof of a crowded house we are told, 'While they all watched, the man got up, picked up his mat, and hurried away. They were all completely amazed and praised God, saying, "We have never seen anything like this!"' (Mark 2:12, GNB).

15. Reincarnation or eternal life?

In New Age thinking life is a series of reincarnations. Through these man is supposed to learn many lessons. (This is dealt with more fully elsewhere in the book.) Christians affirm that we only have one life to live on earth and that that is terminated by death and judgment. However, for the Christian, death means life, not death – that is the incredible paradox of the Christian Gospel. Those who have looked on death in its stark reality are aware of how it seems – so final; so complete; so irreversible! Nothing looks more dead than death. For those who have despised or dismissed the Gospel of Christ, death is an exit without an entrance; an end with no new beginning; a tragedy with no note of triumph; a departure that never has a home-coming; a darkness for which there is no dawn. But for the Christian, death cannot touch the glorious thing which is ours in fellowship with Jesus. Death cannot touch the onward-marching purposes of God. The Christian Church is the only society on earth which never loses a member through death. Here on earth is the land where we die, but we are going to the land of the living where death does not exist any more.

Why on earth would we settle for reincarnation when we can have resurrection to eternal life through Jesus Christ our Lord – with a new body ultimately in a new heaven and a new earth?

11

The Real New Age

New Age is a term which is increasingly being used in all kinds of contexts – the worlds of fashion, architecture, politics, among others. This can lead to confusion in understanding and response. I have no doubt that having read thus far in this book you are under no misapprehension about the context in which we have been addressing the issue. It has clearly been in a religious and spiritual sense. Our concern has been to distinguish the true from the false; the real from the bogus; the light from the darkness; the actual from the pretend and the deceitful. The Christian Gospel has its content and substance based on fact, which will stand the weight of investigation, clinically and carefully carried out, as well as on the reality of human experience. It will be helpful to explore the content of the good news about the real New Age.

Euaggelion: Good News

Euaggelion is the word which is translated 'good news' in the New Testament. Perhaps more familiarly to Christians *Euaggelion* is translated 'Gospel'. It is the heart and centre of the Christian faith. The fact that *euaggelion* occurs seventy-two times in the New Testament (of which fifty-four occurrences are in the Letters of Paul) is evidence of how important and central good news is to what Christians believe. The four Gospels (Matthew, Mark, Luke and John) give information about the good news, whereas Paul makes clear the implications of that good news for us. To the greatest of Christian missionaries Christianity was essentially 'good news'. It involves and includes certain things:

1. The good news of truth

The *Euaggelion* is 'the good news of truth' (see Galatians 2:5, 14). After Jesus came it was no longer necessary to speculate about God. Substance and certainty had now come. With the coming of Jesus the time of groping after the meaning of life was over. Now there was something real, substantial and firm to build life on – something which would bear man's weight when he needed to lean on it or commit himself to it. Christianity was never meant to present man with a series of problems but with an armoury of certainties. The German poet Goethe exclaimed, 'Tell me of your certainties, I have doubts enough of my own.'[1]

G. K. Chesterton once said that the difference between the modern generation and the generation which went before was that the older generation had seen things in terms of black and white, whereas the modern generation saw them in terms of an indeterminate grey. Christians have a heritage of truth which is firm, clear and absolute. This is real good news.

2. The good news of hope

The *euaggelion* is 'the good news of hope' (see Colossians 1:5). Of the three Christian virtues of love, joy and peace, love may be the greatest but hope is shortest in supply. The man who builds his life with the materials which human effort supplies has no alternative but to despair of himself and the world in which he lives. In previous centuries, when visionaries drew their pictures of the future, they usually described an earthly paradise where everyone's needs were supplied and war was a thing of the past. But most twentieth-century prophets are prophets of doom, not of hope:

we need think only of George Orwell's *Nineteen-Eighty-Four*, Aldous Huxley's *Brave New World*, Anthony Burgess's *A Clockwork Orange*, and Neville Shute's *On the Beach*. In *On the Beach* a nuclear war has wiped out civilisation in the Northern Hemisphere, and radioactive dust is drifting southwards, inexorably dealing out to all men radiation sickness, death and oblivion, when one of the characters, Mary, cries out, 'But there's got to be hope.'[2] Left to his own devices – with all his tenacity, expertise and optimism – man has no hope, but when he properly realises what the Christian good news means he is filled with hope for himself and for the world.

3. *The good news of peace*

The *euaggelion* is 'the good news of peace' (see Ephesians 6:15). As long as man continues to try to live life alone he is inevitably a split personality. Man was created to be a creature of two worlds. He was intended to be a creature of this visible world of space and time, but he is also a creature who can only be satisfied when the unseen world of spirit and grace becomes real to him. The good news of the Christian Gospel tells us that reality comes when a man surrenders his life to Christ so that his old self dies and the resurrection life of Christ becomes experience for him. The good news of the Gospel of Christ brings to man the possibility of a fully integrated personality where the old unhappy tensions are ended. Christian peace is not the absence of trouble but the presence of true well-being in God.

4. *The good news of God's promise*

The *euaggelion* is 'the good news of God's promise' (see Ephesians 3:6). Jesus brought the good news that God is not like the gods of paganism – capricious and threatening – but a God who is just and merciful, loving and truthful. God is a God of faithful promise. That does not remove obligation from man – for a promise brings its obligation as much as a threat does – but now it is the obligation to answer to love and not to cringe before vengeance. It is difficult for the Gentile, non-Jewish heart to grasp the wonder of Paul's heart-cry when he says, 'The secret is that by means of the gospel the Gentiles have a part with the Jews in God's blessings; they are members of the same body and share in the promise that God made through Christ Jesus' (Ephesians 3:6, GNB). So Gentiles as well as Jews are recipients of God's favour because of his Son Jesus.

5. *The good news of immortality*

The *euaggelion* is 'the good news of immortality' (see 2 Timothy 1:10). In the face of the devastating reality of death the pagan was filled not only with sorrow but also with fear. For him death was the ultimate statistic; the ultimate finality; he had no hope at all. One of the saddest letters which has come down to us through history is an ordinary, simple papyrus letter from a mother to a couple whose little child had died: 'Irene to Taonnophris and Philo, good comfort. I was as sorry and wept over the departed one as I wept for Didymus. All things that were fitting I did . . . But all the same in the face of such things *there is nothing that anyone can do.*'[3] That was the characteristic and inevitable pagan outlook in the face of death. But the Christian Gospel heralds the reality that death is not the end of life, but the end of the beginning of life. Death is not departure into annihilation but the departure to be forever with God.

One December day in Edinburgh in 1666 Hugh Mackail, youngest and bravest of the so-called 'Covenanting preachers', was brought before his judges and condemned to the scaffold. They gave him four days to live, then the soldiers led the young man back to the Tolbooth. Many of the watching crowd were weeping as he went – so young he seemed, so terrible his coming fate. But in his own eyes no tears were seen; there was no trace of self-pity or regret on the radiant, eager face of this young Galahad of the cross. 'Trust in God!' he cried, and his eyes were shining – 'Trust in God!' Then, suddenly catching a glimpse of a friend among the crowd, 'Good news,' he cried, 'good news! I am within four days' journey of enjoying the sight of Jesus Christ!'[4]

We are to gaze upon that one face which has haunted the dreams of humanity since the day when God walked with men in Galilee, the head that once was crowned with thorns and is crowned with glory now. Death? What is death, if that is beyond it?

6. *The good news of the risen Christ*

The *euaggelion* is 'the good news of the risen Christ' (see 1 Corinthians 15:1–7; 2 Timothy 2:8). The good news which Christianity brings is that we do not worship and serve a dead hero; a figure in a book who lived and died; a man of history who was but now is not. We live with a living presence. We have not been left only with a pattern to copy and an example to follow; we are left with a constant companion of our way. We have the assurance in the good news of Christianity that:

> Death cannot keep his prey,
> Jesus, my Saviour;
> He tore the bars away,
> Jesus, my Lord
> Up from the grave He arose,
> With a mighty triumph o'er His foes;
> He arose a victor from the dark domain,
> And He lives forever with His saints to reign:
> He arose! Hallelujah! Christ arose![5]
> Christ is risen from death, the tomb is empty,
>   and he is alive for ever more.

7. *The good news of salvation*

The *euaggelion* is 'the good news of salvation' (see Ephesians 1:13). It is news of that power which wins us forgiveness for past sin, freedom from present sin, and strength to give us confidence that in the future we will conquer sin whose nature is yet unknown. It is good news of victory.

It is never easy to face the truth about human nature. A contemporary writer, William Golding, in his book *The Lord of the Flies*, does not spare us from facing the reality of what human nature is really like. For too long we 'have never looked further than the rash appearing on the skin'; it is time we began to look 'for the root of the disease instead of describing the symptoms'. So through his writings he lifts the lid and peers inside. He is not concerned with man on the outside: what man would like to be and what he tries to be in front of other people. He is concerned, as God is, with what man is really like in the depths of his being, in the secret places of his heart. He shows us – and who can doubt its validity? – that beneath the surface of our rationality there is a 'seething cauldron of untamed desire'.[6] When we see this picture, our immediate and inevitable response is to try to talk ourselves out of it and explain it away. We talk about inhibitions, complexes, twists in our nature, mistakes we make, and the unpredictability of our temperament. The one thing we will not do, so often, is to use the word the Bible uses and so often Jesus Christ himself used: 'sin'. Frequently we hear the protest: 'I don't understand this concept of sin. I don't know what you mean.' However, over many years it is my experience that no one has any real problem about this concept. Everyone knows what it is to be selfish, to lie, hate, steal, cheat, lust, criticise and judge other people.

The reason why the word 'sin' is so unpopular is that it is too personal. Once I accept the concept of sin, I have to face up to the fact that I am responsible for my actions. I am guilty, and need to be forgiven. Yet sin is the real problem – and this is why Jesus Christ taught so much and did so much about sin. In fact he unquestionably saw it as the result of man's crying need for God. He saw it as corrupting and spoiling the life of every person born into the world. This is why Jesus came fundamentally – not just to show us what God is like, but to 'save his people from their sins' (Matthew 1:21, GNB). The people he came to save were not bad; on the contrary, they appeared good. They were not pagan; they were religious. They did not disregard God; they were devoted to him. But Jesus knew that unless the diagnosis of man was known and accepted, and unless the surgeon's knife could do its work, the cancer of sin would spread and kill.

The humanist has a silly optimism that man is able to cope with himself and with the bewildering problems which confront the world, provided he is not shackled with the immature creeds of religion. However, humanism flourishes normally only in intellectual circles where it is easy to be idealistic and doctrinaire about life. As a pastor, I have been faced constantly with complex and destructive human and domestic problems. In this ordinary world of needy men and women, although many strange beliefs exist, it is rare to encounter a convinced humanist. Once you step out of an intellectual greenhouse into the fierce storms of everyday life, you are forced to be realistic about human nature and that includes being realistic about sin – by whatever name you refer to it.

Christianity is the good news that sin has been confronted and dealt with in Jesus Christ – and we become free from its power and penalty with our ears and not with our hands. We can be free not on the basis of what we are able to do, but on the basis of who Jesus was and what Jesus did. Christianity begins not with a big imperative 'do', but with a conclusive and comprehensive 'done'.

Repentance is the key on man's side. The Greek word translated 'repentance' is *metanoia* which meant originally an 'afterthought': often a second thought shows that the first thought was wrong, and so the word came to mean 'a change of mind'! But, if a man is honest, a change of mind demands a change of action. Repentance, then, must involve both a change of mind and a change of action. A man may change his mind and come to see that his actions were wrong, but be so much in love with his old ways that he will not change them. A man may mend his ways but his mind remains the same, changing only because of fear or prudence. True repentance involves both a change of mind and a change of action.

One of the Hebrew words translated 'repentance' is *shob* which means 'to turn back' – in our experience making a U-turn. So, repentance is more than feeling sorry or having regrets and remorse for what we have done. Speaking of Peter's call to repentance in the sermon preached on the day of Pentecost (Acts 2:38) Dr Jim Packer says: 'Peter was prescribing not a formal posture of regret for the Crucifixion, but a total renunciation of independence as a way of living and total submission to the rule of the risen Lord.'[7]

However difficult it may be to perceive this at first sight, repentance is the secret of the joy-filled life. It has nothing to do with earning favour; achieving a standard; or becoming good. It has everything to do with opening the door to all that God has done and will do for us – for grace is God's response to man's repentance.

Every letter Paul ever wrote (and which has been included in the New Testament) begins and ends with grace. Grace is the essence and centre of the good news of Christianity. Grace is a lovely thing. The Greek word for grace is *charis*, and *charis* can mean physical beauty – everything which is contained in the word charm. Grace always moves in the realm of winsomeness, loveliness, attractiveness, beauty and charm. There are some Christian words which carry (of necessity) the atmosphere of sternness and severity. Grace, however, has about it (in the Christian sense) the idea of surpassing beauty so that the human heart when it properly understands can only bow down in wondering adoration before it.

As well as the idea of beauty, grace always has about it the idea of a gift which is completely free and entirely undeserved. The ideas of grace and merit are mutually exclusive and completely contradictory. No one can ever earn grace; it can only be humbly, gratefully and adoringly received. It is a gift given out of the sheer generosity of the giver's heart, without effort on the receiver's part. So no one need ever attempt to qualify for the grace of God – the mercy, love, power and providence of God can only be gladly accepted.

The link between man's sin and God's grace is faith. The position of Paul in the New Testament is straightforward: Accept the position that the good things you do are either able to earn or contribute towards your salvation, and you have accepted the position that man by his unaided efforts can acquire merit in the sight of God; and simply to state that possibility is to obliterate the fact and the need of grace. But accept the position that all is of grace, that all is the generous gift of God, and nothing further is needed. To bring in anything further is to deny the full sufficiency and the full adequacy of grace.

Paul himself made the great discovery that divine grace needs no human addition to be effective for salvation.

During World War I any pilot who got himself into a spin would crash. Lord Cherwell, the sometime Professor of Physics at Oxford University and scientific adviser to Winston Churchill during World War II, studied this problem and managed to convert the aerodynamics of a spinning dive into a mathematical formula. He agreed that if the pilot were to act in a certain way on the basis of his formula, he could correct the spin. The commandant of one aerodrome was interested but felt it unreasonable to expect any pilot to put it to the test on the strength of a mere formula jotted down on a piece of paper. Professor Cherwell said, 'Teach me to fly and I will prove to you that the theory is true.' They did, and he did. Within three weeks of qualifying he flew to a great height, deliberately put the plane into a spin, and demonstrated that the formula worked. Not content with that, he insisted on going up again and showed that it also worked in an anti-clockwise direction.[8]

Such is the nature of true faith: it believes the good news of the Gospel of Christ, puts it to the test and discovers that

grace is not only free but real and effective. So Paul cries,
'God puts people right through their faith in Jesus Christ.
God does this to all who believe in Christ, because there is
no difference at all: everyone has sinned and is far away
from God's saving presence. But by the free gift of God's
grace all are put right with him through Christ Jesus, who
sets them free' (Romans 3:22–24, GNB).

Long ago John the Baptist came proclaiming: 'It is not
enough to repent and be baptized that your sin might be
cleansed. If you want to go on in the Christian life you need
to meet two other people – God the Son, and God the Holy
Spirit.'[9] For us, having met God the Father and God the
Son, it is necessary to meet God the Holy Spirit in a living
and dynamic way. There is a remarkable story of a ship
which ran into difficulties in a storm in the Atlantic Ocean.
It eventually went down and the small crew took to the
life-boat. The days became weeks and they drifted helpless
and undetected. Unknown to them they were given up as
'lost with all hands' and searches were called off. The food
they had was running low, but it was their water that gave
out first. One morning, early, they saw a ship and signalled
to her with their shirts. She saw them and steamed towards
them. As she towered above it was clear that rescue was
going to be difficult. By this time the shipwrecked crew
were so thirsty and weak that even rescue was not their first
need. They desperately needed water. As their rescuers
prepared to get them aboard all they could cry was, 'Water!
Water!' To their cry came the response: 'Dip your bucket
over the side!' On the face of it that seemed like a cruel and
despicable joke. However, apparently they were drifting
off the mouth of the Amazon River which pushes its fresh
water right out into the Atlantic. They were actually drifting in the very water that they needed so desperately; all
they needed was to dip their buckets over the side.[10]

In a strange way that could easily be a picture of the
contemporary Church in the United Kingdom. So often the
Church is seen to be drifting – with no direction or sense of
purpose – not going anywhere. So often she has been seen

as a life-boat of dying people huddled together for corporate protection – a pathetic, feckless congregation of nice people who are victims of misfortune. But long ago, we are told,

> Jesus stood up and said in a loud voice, 'Whoever is thirsty should come to me and drink. As the scripture says, "Whoever believes in me, streams of life-giving water will pour out from his heart".' Jesus said this about the Spirit, which those who believed in him were going to receive. At that time the Spirit had not yet been given, because Jesus had not been raised to glory.
>
> (John 7:37–39, GNB)

But Jesus has now been glorified: he is the Lord who was dead, now he lives and has ascended to be in the place of authority in the throne-room of the universe.

God's first great gift to man came on that first Christmas morning with the angels declaring his glory and the shepherds discovering his reality. 'For God loved the world so much that he gave his only Son, so that everyone who believes in him may not die, but have eternal life' (John 3:16, GNB). But his second great gift came in the phenomenon of Pentecost so vividly recorded for us by Luke in the Acts of the Apostles. The picture is rather like that of a little child opening his first present on Christmas morning. The gift turns out to be just what he had dreamed about, and what he had felt he so much needed to make life possible and liveable – a train-set from his grandparents. He is enthralled by it and any other presents are ignored – to the dismay of his parents. They had really broken the bank to buy him a bike – but in his enthusiasm and wonder he hadn't even noticed that, even though it had been so difficult to conceal. The train-set is unwrapped and set up and obviously is everything he had ever wanted – at least for a little while. Then it dawns on him that there are more presents, and he sees the bike. His eyes are wide with wonder and he now wants to explore the possibilities of this second gift.

The good news of the Christian faith is that there is another 'present' for us – the third person in the Trinity, the Holy Spirit. Through the New Testament, indeed, the Holy Spirit is referred to as a gift. I can remember years ago a great missionary warrior standing in our pulpit and saying, 'When I became a Christian, I changed from being a hell-deserving sinner into becoming a helpless saint.' Norman Grubb was to discover that God not only provides his Son for hell-deserving sinners, but also his spirit for helpless saints. We don't deserve him – and we cannot earn, win or recruit him – but God gives his Spirit to us.

In his final teaching to his disciples in the Upper Room on that momentous eve of his crucifixion Jesus spoke freely and powerfully about his Spirit to those vulnerable, apprehensive and broken-hearted disciples of his (John 13–17). He told them seven things about his Spirit then:

(i) The self-same Spirit who had been given to him at his baptism in the Jordan River would be given to them.

(ii) The Holy Spirit would be to them all that he had been to him.

(iii) The Holy Spirit would be to them all that he, the Son, had been to them – and more.

(iv) The Holy Spirit would be *in* them, as the Son had been *with* them – so the restrictions of space and time would be gone.

(v) They would gain in the Holy Spirit more than they would lose in the departure of Christ.

(vi) The Holy Spirit would be 'another of the same kind' as he was and, through the Holy Spirit's indwelling, Christ would live in them.

(vii) The Holy Spirit's mission was to glorify the Son by taking the things of Christ and making them available to them. So the fruit of the Holy Spirit would produce the character of Christ in thcm (and us!) and the gifts of the Holy Spirit would bestow the conduct of Christ on them (and us!).

Such is the incredible wonder of the Holy Spirit's person and ministry that what Jesus made possible by his death on the cross the Holy Spirit wants to make thrillingly actual in the lives of ordinary men and women.

So our responsibility to display the character of Christ to a disbelieving world becomes a possibility – not through greater and more strenuous self-effort, but through the generous ministry of the Holy Spirit within us creating his fruit. So also our responsibility to demonstrate the conduct of Christ to a broken, needy world becomes a possibility – again not through greater enthusiasm on our part but through the gracious ministry of the Holy Spirit upon us conveying his gifts. So the world can see the character and conduct of Christ – what he is really like and what he really can do – through ordinary people like us, not because we are good but because he is gracious.

So the real good news continues of God's purpose and provision for us. For in all of this it was never God's intention that we should live out these realities on our own. Christianity may be a personal thing, but it is never private. Dr John Mackay of Princeton Theological Seminary in the USA once said, 'We become related to Christ singly but we can never live in Christ solitarily.'[11] Isolation of Christians is the devil's ploy but it was never God's purpose. When Jesus ascended to return to his Father in heaven, it was always God's intention to create a new body on earth which would be able to declare his word to all men, and to demonstrate his power. That new body was born on the day of Pentecost. Now God had a new body on earth – his Church. Jesus has returned to the place from which he came taking with him his human nature and experience. His place on earth has been taken over by the Holy Spirit who has no body but lives in Christians. As a Christian I am called to be a living, functioning member of that body – and God has a specific, personal work for me here on earth within that body.

The gifts which the Holy Spirit gives have nothing what-ever to do with status or reward but have everything to do with function and relevance. These gifts are given by God to enable his new body on earth – the Church – to function properly. The great theologian John Owen reminds us that, 'gifts proceed solely from the regal office and power of Christ. They are all given unto and distributed for the good of the Church, but they are effects only of His Kingly power.'[12] Another theologian of this century, Emil Brunner, writing in *The Misunderstanding of the Church*, says,

> One thing is extremely important: that *all* minister, and that nowhere is to be perceived a separation or even merely a distinction between those who do, and those who do not minister, between the active and passive members of the Body of Christ, between those who give and those who receive. There exists in the *Ekklesia* a universal duty and right of service, a universal readiness to serve, and at the same time the greatest possible differentiation of function.[13]

Someone once put into verse the awesome consequences of trying to go it alone:

> O crooked, lovely forest tree,
> And crooked because lonely;
> If only comrades two or three
> Could share your lone monotony,
> How very different life would be . . .[14]

Just so – the desire of God is that we would discover and develop deep, real and significant relationships within his new body on earth, the Church. Fellowship and family are powerful, practical New Testament concepts. They are not regarded as optional extras, but fundamental obligations to living the Jesus life in the power of the Holy Spirit. When man gets out of fellowship with God, he will inevitably sooner rather than later get out of fellowship with his brother man. So Genesis 3 is quickly followed by Genesis 4: the husband and wife, Adam and Eve, are alienated and estranged from God in chapter 3 through their disobedience and rebellion; soon afterwards in chapter 4 this climate of estrangement from God created by the parents leads to alienation and estrangement between the children, Cain and Abel – resulting in the murder of Abel by Cain. When Jesus comes, however, he is concerned not simply to restore man back to fellowship with God but also back to fellowship and relationship with man. So it is that the Church exists – to fulfil this God-given function.

Not only are loneliness and isolation gone for ever but in an uncertain and apprehensive world it is good to know that Jesus is not only a prophet (as he is portrayed in the Gospels so powerfully); priest (as he is portrayed in the letters of the New Testament so plainly); but also King (as he is proclaimed in Revelation). He is in the throne-room of the universe and he has ultimate control. History is *his story*. The world and the future are not in the hands of the politician or the dictator or the scientist or the terrorist or the madman: they are in his powerful hands. The Book of Revelation has been written to show that however deep the trouble might be God is on the throne; right will triumph at last; and wrong will be conquered for ever. Revelation really draws back the curtain (*apokalupsis*) and gives us a peep behind the scenes. It is like going backstage in the theatre and seeing who is pulling the ropes – who is really in charge. Revelation is a theology of power – and that power belongs to God. In a world where there seems to be a daily record of violence, hatred, filth, guilt and cruelty, this is really good news. Revelation not only completes the Bible but it also brings God's redemption to a happy conclusion. Without 'Revelation' the Bible would leave you in mid-air. It would be rather like reading a detective story and discovering that someone had torn out the last few pages – so leaving you terribly frustrated. Many modern novels and plays do just that – significantly they have no real ending; there is no meaning or conclusion. But not so with God's book and God's heart. Life begins in a garden and ends in a garden city; life begins with a tree of life forbidden and ends with a tree of life available. To read the first three chapters of Genesis and the last three chapters of Revelation is to

find a remarkable correspondence. It is not the fictional
Mills & Boon novels or the writings of Barbara Cartland
that have the right and authority to declare that all will be
well in the end; it is the factual, historical reality of the
'Revelation' of the heart of God that has this right and
authority. Those whom God has redeemed and loosed
from their sins by the sacrifice of his Son and made his kings
and priests face a future bright with hope and shining in its
reality. To read Revelation is to be like a solicitor reading
the details of a will and stating what is going to come to you
in Christ.

'The great divine far-off event to which the whole creation is moving' is the return of Jesus Christ to this earth. We
are today living between the two great events of history –
the first coming (Christmas) of Christ and his return. This
latter is the next great event on the state of history. For this
reason the Bible lays great emphasis upon it. One out of
every thirty verses in the Bible mentions this hope (1,200
times in the Old Testament and over 300 times in the New
Testament). There are approximately the same number of
references to the return of Jesus to earth in the New
Testament as there are references to his cross. Significantly, for every mention of the first Advent of Christ –
Christmas – there are eight mentions of his second Advent.
In the 216 chapters of the New Testament there are 318
references to it. Whole books of the New Testament (1 and
2 Thessalonians, for example) and whole chapters (Matthew 24; Mark 13; Luke 21) give special emphasis to it. It is
the theme of the prophets of the Old Testament:

> It was concerning this salvation that the prophets made careful
> search and investigation, and they prophesied about this gift
> which God would give you. They tried to find out when the time
> would be and how it would come. This was the time to which
> Christ's Spirit was pointing, in predicting the sufferings that
> Christ would have to endure and the glory that would follow.
>   (1 Peter 1:10–11, GNB)

The angels bore witness to the first Advent, one of their
number intruding unexpectedly into the pastoral night-shift

of the shepherds on duty in Bethlehem's fields, and dramatically declaring: 'Don't be afraid! I am here with good news for you, which will bring great joy to all the people. This very day in David's town your Saviour was born – Christ the Lord! And this is what will prove it to you: you will find a baby wrapped in strips of cloth and lying in a manger' (Luke 2:10–12, GNB). Suddenly the lone messenger of God was joined by 'a great army of heaven's angels . . . singing praises to God: "Glory to God in the highest heaven, and peace on earth to those with whom he is pleased!"'

The angels also bore witness with equal directness to the second Advent when the apostles were startled by Jesus's ascension: 'Galileans, why are you standing there looking up at the sky? This Jesus, who was taken from you into heaven, will come back in the same way that you saw him go to heaven' (Acts 1:10–11, GNB). Twenty-three of the twenty-seven New Testament books contain references to the return of Christ to this planet. Only four New Testament books (Galatians – written with the specific purpose of correcting the false teaching that it was necessary to obey the Law of Moses in order to be a true Christian – Philemon, 2 and 3 John which are significantly short letters) have no reference to the Second Coming of Christ. When you compare this mass of biblical evidence with the fact that the Lord's Supper is mentioned only seven times, it seems startling that many would be unwilling to neglect Communion and yet would never think nor adjust their lives to the reality of the return of Christ into human history.

Lord Shaftesbury, who could never be charged with sitting in isolated, cloistered cosiness, removed from the pains and pressures of his society, said towards the end of his life, 'I do not think that in the last forty years I have lived one conscious hour that was not influenced by the thought of the Lord's return.'[15] Without doubt, the return of Jesus provided not a doctrine to be debated and discussed but a fact against which the whole of life was to be lived plus the certainty that God is in charge, and that history – however bleak and depressing it may become – is in his control. Undoubtedly this was the attitude of the early Church. They looked back with deep thanksgiving to the cross where Jesus dealt with our sins; they looked up to the heavens where Jesus is seated on the right hand of God the Father Almighty, constantly interceding on our behalf; but they also looked forward to his coming again – and so should we if we are to get our present life and service into perspective. According to the New Testament that return is an event, not a process; and it is personal and in bodily form. It is this event which God intends should have a profoundly practical effect upon the lives that we live within society.

For this reason it is good that we study every word of promise in Scripture and scan the political horizon for any sign that the time of its fulfilment is drawing near – whether that be the unprecedented violence throughout the world; the escalating and frightening moral decline within and among the nations; the political ferment leading towards some form of global unification under a world dictator; or even the restoration of the Jews to their own land, with all the political and moral confusion that has created. The Bible tells us enough about the return of Christ to stimulate and strengthen our faith, even if it does not satisfy our curiosity.

> O Lord, 'tis for Thee, for Thy coming we wait:
> The sky, not the grave, is our goal;
> O, trump of the angel! O voice of the Lord!
> Blessed hope! Blessed rest of my soul![16]

Such was the climate of hope and expectancy; such was the good news grasped and enjoyed which permeated the early Church and influenced its attitudes and activities. So it must be with us.

The Christian, then, is aware that this is the land of the dying; this is where we are bewildered, suffer pain and weakness; this is where we shed tears; this is where disease so often humiliates and degrades us; this is where the ultimate statistic is death. But what of tomorrow's world? The sting of death has now been drawn – our ground of certainty and hope is the resurrection of Jesus and behind that the reality of the love and justice of God. The universe will be transformed – for there is going to be a new heaven and a new earth in the providence of God, and our present experience of heaven and earth will pass away. Death, darkness, pain, suffering, limitation, parting and tears will be gone for ever, never to return. Evil will be no more and perfection will be established, and be the norm. Insecurity will no longer threaten us for nothing will contrive towards it. We will be forever in the presence of God aware of his light in which there is no darkness at all and appreciating his love with all its infinite variety of expression. Indeed, love will reign and God's glory – the brightness and comprehensiveness of his being – will always be seen.

No wonder the message of Christianity is always referred to as Gospel – good news. Fundamentally, it is good news of God in that it showed to men a God the like of whom they had never even dreamed – a God whose heart is love. But it is also good news 'sent by God'. Behind the whole process of man's salvation is God. It was because God loved the world so much that he sent his Son. The good news is *of* God and *from* God.

12

Putting on the Armour

We have, so far, described what the New Age is, where it has come from, what its main emphases are, how it differs from traditional Christian faith and what its strengths and weaknesses are. But how should the reader react? One last piece of the jigsaw needs to be put in place. What is the positive overall Christian response to the New Age movement?

'The New Age Movement grew on what many perceived to be a great spiritual hunger in the West'.[1] 'Cults are the unpaid bills of the church.'[2] It is the Christian's responsibility and privilege to meet that spiritual hunger with food that satisfies. This present generation of the world-wide Christian Church has the great opportunity to discharge that debt, and in the words of the apostle Paul, not to be 'ashamed of the gospel, because it is the power of God for the salvation of everyone who believes' (Romans 1:16, NIV).

The Five-fold Christian Response to the New Age

We should, as Christians, be eager to make the following five-fold response to the New Age as a movement, and to individuals who have been caught up with its teaching.

1. Christians should be concerned with truth

We need to acknowledge, gladly, those areas of New Age teaching that are true. The Christian does not condemn

New Age faith or its intellectual integrity with a *blanket* denial of all that it represents.

For example, as we have seen, the movement is concerned with the preservation of the resources of the created world. Christians should be too. We have been reminded of the creation mandate to order, preserve and rightly use the world's natural resources which has never been withdrawn (Genesis 1:28–30; 9:1–13; and Psalm 8).

> When I consider your heavens,
> the work of your fingers,
> the moon and the stars,
> which you have set in place,
> what is man that you are mindful of him,
> the son of man that you care for him? . . .
> You made him ruler over the works of your hands;
> you put everything under his feet:
> all flocks and herds,
> and the beasts of the field,
> the birds of the air,
> and the fish of the sea,
> all that swim the paths of the seas.
>
> (Psalm 8:3–4, 6–8)

The New Age movement stresses the importance of the body and its care. Right exercise and healthy eating are on its agenda. This should also concern Christians, for our bodies are temples of the Holy Spirit. New Agers seek to promote the cause of world peace. So should Christians, even though we are warned by Jesus that there will be wars and rumours of wars.

The New Age movement calls for a radical transformation within man – a total change of mind in people. While the Christian will not mean the same thing by those words, he or she will, of course, be concerned to work and pray for the radical spiritual transformation of all men and women.

There are other areas, also, that might not at first sight seem to be areas of agreement with Christians. For example, the Christian leaders of the 'Spiritual Counterfeits Project' in America list the following:

> An emphasis on co-operation instead of competition; creativity – Christians often find themselves defending mediocrity and rigidity, instead of encouraging spontaneity and creativity; human potential and positive self-image – people are created in God's image – Christians support human potential and a positive self-image, but not unlimited human potential and not an unflawed self; the Global village – one of the most radical changes in the last twenty years is that we can no longer function as an isolated nation, politically or economically – a crisis in one country affects the whole world. [Witness for example, the movements and crashes on the world stock markets on Black Monday, October 1987, and similar fears on Friday, 13th October 1989.][3]

However much we stress the areas where Christians and New Agers can agree, we have also to identify those areas and ideas where truth has been distorted, where people's minds have been deceived, and as a result individuals are acting in response to delusions and lies.

One example will suffice. On 31st December 1986, in groups and centres around the world, a 'World Healing Day' was observed with the following meditation included. The leader declared:

> I am co-creator with God, and it is a new Heaven that comes, as the Good Will of God is expressed on Earth through me . . . In Truth, I am the Christ of God . . . God is all and all is God . . . I am the Light of the World . . . and now from the Light of the World, the one Presence and Power of the Universe responds . . . I am seeing the salvation of the planet before my very eyes, as all false beliefs and error patterns are dissolved . . . [4]

The appropriate Christian response to the lies and deception of the New Age is the proclamation and propagation of biblical truth. Effective Christian teaching is essential. We live in a world where, for the most part in the West, children are growing up in complete ignorance of Christian knowledge and ideas. If children and young people are not taught the truth of Christianity at home or school or in Christian churches where will they receive basic Christian instruction? Nowhere! It is the increasing experience of ministers, clergy and Christian leaders that adults are coming to a living faith in God and Jesus with the most rudimentary understanding of the Christian Gospel. We live in days when we dare make no assumptions about an individual's understanding of what we mean by God, man, sin, Jesus, salvation, new life, the Bible, forgiveness, the future, etc.

Let me give one or two illustrations. The New Age believes in a pantheistic view of God. God is everywhere, and man is God. The Christian affirms a personal God who is both within us through the indwelling of the Holy Spirit, and also far beyond us and sovereign in the world. In theological terms, the Christian speaks of God as both immanent and transcendent. God is distinct from and above his creation, and yet day by day sustains all he has made. Again, New Age writers distinguish the historical person of Jesus of Nazareth from the Christ. Jesus, they say, is not the God-man but one of the many God-realised masters. 'The Christ is that life, love, intelligence, and energetic power which maintains creation in existence. It is within each one of us. Christ's message becomes, "I am attuned, I am one with the whole".'[5]

As we have seen, there are many fundamental conflicts between the teaching of the New Age and the truth of Christianity. We need to understand both, and to be concerned for the truth. Jesus taught us that we are not only to *know* the truth, but also to *do* the truth. One aspect of 'doing the truth' is to discover where New Age teaching and influence is found and expose it for what it is.

It has been my increasing experience, in researching for this book, that New Age influence and information will be found in our daily papers, especially the intellectual quality ones, and in the weekend magazine supplements. It will be associated with the pop culture, record reviews, advertisements for perfumes and business proficiency courses. We have also seen that New Age thinking has invaded the Church, and will pervade our schools and almost every area of public and corporate life.

To sum up: the Christian is concerned with the truth. We discern where we are able to identify areas of truth within the New Age movement. We expose those areas where Christian terms are used but given a very different meaning, causing others to be misled. We also see the need to teach the historic truth of the Christian faith to the vast majority of children and adults growing up in today's world who are untaught and ignorant about God.

2. *Christians should be concerned with the right use of the human mind*

The mind of man is a battlefield when, today, the forces of truth and error wage war. Basilea Schlink reveals how this battle for the mind is being waged:

> Behind the facade of healthy eating and fitness, New Age programmes usually include the following practices, which are nothing more than variations on Eastern occult techniques: meditation – yoga and relaxation therapies – hypnosis – psychic healing – visualisation and positive thinking. The latter two are based on the assumption that the mind through suggestion can accomplish and create anything that it believes it can.[6]

A lady phoned me one evening concerned about advice given to her. She had been going to yoga classes. She had been told by Christian friends that she should cease to go. She could not understand why, especially when she felt better. I explained to her that while the physical elements of yoga could benefit her body, she was also required to empty her mind of her thoughts and then allow any phrase, word or mantra that was fed to her to make itself at home in her mind. She began to understand the potential danger she faced. Her mind was the faculty given her by God with which she could direct her own life. She was unwittingly surrendering that right and responsibility to others. There was a battle for her mind. I believe she put the telephone down an enlightened and reassured woman.

Basilea Schlink points out that children and young people are being influenced by New Age ideas through a barrage of fantasy games, videos, films, audio cassettes, comic books, literature, party games and toys. Seven of the ten most popular films in the history of film-making are classified as fantasy. Heading the chart is *E.T.* which has given rise to a whole new youth culture. *Star Wars* is in second place. Seventy-five per cent of box-office successes have fantasy themes. Fantasy books are best-sellers, with editions running into millions. Hundreds of titles are already on the market, almost always presenting some form of occultism (such as communication with the dead, conjuring spirits, clairvoyance, telepathy and levitating objects by the power of thought) and featuring sorcerers, witches and magicians.[7]

We believe that every child has a right to have his or her imagination stirred and to enjoy a fair dose of mystery and wonder. After all, isn't that the special world of children? What is happening, however, is that impressionable minds are being fed with a potentially dangerous overdose of fantasy and magic. Children and young people need to grow up in a world where they are able to discern and know what is true. They need to know what absolute truth is: what the unchanging standards in life are.

It was Jesus himself who declared, 'I thank thee, Father, Lord of heaven and earth, that thou hast hidden these things from the wise and understanding and revealed them to babes; yea, Father, for such was thy gracious will. All things have been delivered to me by my Father; and no one knows the Son except the Father, and no one knows the Father except the Son and any one to whom the Son chooses to reveal him' (Matthew 11:25–27, RSV). No wonder St Paul commends and encourages Timothy's example of knowing and reading the Scriptures from childhood.

We must be concerned with the battle for truth, and the battle for the mind of people in today's world. What we read, and see, and hear and experience will either rightly teach or poisonously deceive our minds.

3. Christians are to be concerned with freedom and wholeness

God has given us all things richly to enjoy, and the Christian life should never be narrow, negative or dull. We are exhorted to live life to the full and to be whole and free people. We believe that this freedom and wholeness are found only in and through Jesus. It was the claim of Jesus that 'if the Son makes you free, you will be free indeed' (John 8:36, RSV). Such freedom is found in the truth of Jesus. The question therefore arises as to how can we help people who have become entangled in some way or other with the New Age movement, who, thinking they were finding fulfilment, have in fact fallen into bondage.

We need to understand that New Agers are concerned with principles, but the Christian is concerned with a person. New Agers have a contrastingly different view of Salvation and forgiveness from the Christian view. For the New Ager there is no forgiveness or mercy in his belief in Karma. There is only the hope or the fear of a higher or lower form of life. But Christians are concerned with Christ – a person; and only a person can forgive.

We must direct people in need to understand the finished work of Jesus, and the complete transformation that is possible through him, rather than the counterfeit transformation that the New Ager seeks through himself. As Paul proclaimed, 'if any one is in Christ, he is a new creation; the old has gone, the new has come!' (2 Corinthians 5:17, NIV). Again, Paul wrote to the Christians at Colossae that God the Father had qualified them to share in the inheritance of the saints in the kingdom of light: 'For he has rescued us from the dominion of darkness and brought us into the kingdom of the Son he loves, in whom we have redemption, the forgiveness of sins' (Colossians 1:12–14, NIV).

Because the Christian is in Christ, Satan, our spiritual adversary, need not ensnare us again. We have been set free and given a new start. The curse and bondage which a man or woman discovered through the New Age movement and its occult teaching have been broken.

Humanly speaking, we cannot effect this release from the guilt of sin and the reality of being made clean within. But it can be made real through the work of the Holy Spirit of God, and the believing prayers of God's people.

We need to rely completely upon the work and ministry of the Holy Spirit when we seek to bring freedom to those bound by the New Age. We shall need the gifts of the Spirit to bring deliverance to those who have been ensnared. We shall need the gift of knowledge, the word of wisdom and the spirit of discernment in order to understand what evil spirits are controlling the person to whom we are ministering. We shall need to discern how best we may minister to an individual. Do they need physical healing or deliverance from psychic powers? Have they been involved with the occult, caught up in yoga or dabbled with tarot cards? The right diagnosis, as revealed by the Holy Spirit, will lead to the right spiritual medicine being offered. There will be the need to lead a person to renounce what once they believed, and to repent of activities and attitudes they held.

In the same way, a Christian must refuse to dabble with the occult or be fascinated by the weird. We are reminded that we are called to 'put off' all thoughts, actions and attitudes that do not honour Christ, and to put on all that exalts the Saviour, and makes more powerful the work and ministry of the Holy Spirit in our lives.

Throughout this book we have been making the point that the New Age movement is an unholy alliance of Eastern religions, secular humanism and the occult. This point was again reinforced by an article in the *Sunday*

Times (29th October 1989) in an article by Kate Saunders in the 'Style and Society' section. In her review of the New Age movement (which also included reference to clothes and perfumes) Ms Saunders quoted Ian Howarth who runs the 'Cult Information Centre', whose work is to educate people about the possible harmful side-effects of the cults: 'Ex-members often feel they have been deceived and exploited. I would say the whole New Age movement is revolving around practices associated with the occult, and riddled with links with cult groups.'

It might be easy to make light of the occult element in the New Age. I happen to be writing these words on 31st October – Hallowe'en Night. The Evangelical Alliance has reminded Christians, in its first Action Agenda paper for its church representatives, of the facts about Hallowe'en and the occult:

> Hallowe'en [says the Report] grew out of the Druid celebration of Samhuinn, Lord of the Dead on 1 November. On the eve of this festival, it was believed that he called together wicked spirits that in the past year had been condemned to dwell in the bodies of dead animals . . . It is estimated that there are some 30,000 practising witches in the United Kingdom; occultist groups are currently running six telephone helplines; and more than 100 occult magazines are available in Britain. Many openly recruit teenage volunteers. MPs are becoming increasingly concerned about reports of ritual abuse and sacrifice, and the police and social workers are dealing with several cases of ritual child abuse and sacrifice in Satanic covens, whose membership has multiplied one hundredfold in the past 15 years. We also know that one in four religious books published in Britain in 1988 was on the theme of the occult. The occult is a major part of the New Age scene.[8]

Behind all this so-called harmless activity is the person and work of the devil or Satan. The Bible reveals Satan as a spiritual personality who is able to deceive, not just a vague evil force that has some influence (Genesis 3:1, 2 Corinthians 11:3). Satan is the ultimate source of all lies (John

8:44). He blinds the minds and understanding of people to the truth of the Gospel (2 Corinthians 4:4). He will falsely accuse Christians (Revelation 12:10). He has the ability to present himself as good in the guise of an angel of light (2 Corinthians 11:14) and he would seek to destroy Christians through his work just as a roaring lion would (1 Peter 5:8).

Even though Satan is strong, Christians rejoice to affirm that Jesus Christ is stronger. Jesus appeared on earth, suffered death on the cross and was raised to life by God the Father in order to destroy all the works of the devil, and to rob him of his power. Satan is alive and kicking, but his power has been broken. His days have been numbered, and his future destiny and destruction assured.

As Christians we are called to put on the whole armour of God in the fight in which we are involved. Paul outlines the nature of the spiritual conflict for us in Ephesians 6:

> Put on the full armour of God so that you can take your stand against the devil's schemes. For our struggle is not against flesh and blood, but against the rulers, against the authorities, against the powers of this dark world and against the spiritual forces of evil in the heavenly realms. Therefore put on the full armour of God, so that when the day of evil comes, you may be able to stand your ground, and after you have done everything, to stand.
>
> (Ephesians 6:11–13, NIV)

Paul then reminds us of the individual pieces of spiritual equipment that God has given for the spiritual battle – the belt of truth, the breastplate of righteousness, the sandals of peace, the shield of faith, the helmet of salvation, and the sword of the Spirit, which is the word of God, and finally, the weapon of always praying in the Spirit. It should be at once abundantly obvious that each piece of this armour is essential in the conflict Christians have with the New Age movement.

4. Christians must be concerned with evangelism

There is a further response that Christians are called to make to the New Age. It is to share the good news of the Christian faith with those who are attracted to its teaching. We are not only called upon to deny error, but also to share the truth.

If we need but one reason for doing so, let me remind you that I can find no evidence of any Christian ever having had the opportunity to share the truth of Jesus with a person like Shirley MacLaine. If she had become a committed Christian, and not an ardent New Ager, one wonders what difference there would have been both in her own life and in those of others.

It is clear that Christians will need to do their homework, and understand the New Age. We shall need to be relevant and use appropriate thought forms. For example, we shall need to speak about the *truth* of the Incarnation – of Jesus becoming man etc., rather than the *error* of reincarnation, which lies at the heart of New Age teaching. We shall need to build bridges into New Age lives, rather than erect barriers against people with whom we don't agree.

As an outstanding and very practical example of just such evangelism, we can study with much profit the account of Paul's visit to Athens in Acts 17:16–31. Athens was a city given over to idolatry, and a panoply of gods. Paul took his time to look around the city, and understand what people were thinking. He stood and looked and listened. He discovered common ground – the Altar to an Unknown God. I can tell you about him, says St Paul, and proceeds to speak about Jesus. Paul was able to make the distinction between the people he was speaking to, and the religious philosophy they embraced. He loved the first, and disassociated himself from the second. He deliberately became familiar with their culture and religious background. He clearly related the Gospel in a way they could grasp. That is our task also.

For example, we can teach about the need of regeneration, rather than the false gospel of reincarnation. The New Ager speaks a lot about personal transformation and personal affirmation. The Christian is able to testify to transformation through Jesus and the affirmation and acceptance (justification and sanctification) that are possible through the mercy and grace of God and the work of the Lord Jesus Christ. We can speak of forgiveness through a person rather than the uncertain hope of a better life in the hereafter.

All this may seem a formidable task. But we have the work of the Holy Spirit to aid us, and the weapon of prayer – our own and those of others to encourage and support us. We can pray along the lines of John 16:8–11 – affirming that it is the work of the Spirit to convict the world of sin, righteousness and judgment to come. We can pray that the Holy Spirit will lead the person caught up in – or attracted by – the New Age to the confession of their sin, and of repentance towards God.

As Charles Stronmer, a former New Ager and now a full-time Christian worker, will testify, we should pray for the power of God to work mightily in that person's life. Not only is there likely to be confusion in his or her mind, but there will often be the evidence of evil spirits seeking to take possession, or even of their actually having done so. We shall need to pray for the power of Jesus to deliver and set such a person free.

We can pray that the Holy Spirit will make Jesus real because he is the answer. This may mean that at times we have lovingly to confront a person with the truth. We must pray that they will accept the reality of a loving God who longs to forgive them. We can pray that God will reveal the supernatural forces that have control of their lives. We can pray that they will become open to Christianity, and that understanding and compassionate Christians will draw alongside them and encourage them. We can pray that we shall know the appropriate good Christian literature to share with them. Most people caught up in the New Age are intellectually sharp and need to have substantial and relevant answers.

Basilea Schlink echoes this call to prayer in her little booklet 'New Age' in a simple and direct way:

> 'Save souls! Rescue them!' is the cry in these dawning end times when Satan continues to extend his rule. God wants to rescue many more who are in Satan's grip and we are called to assist Him. This is something each of us can do through our prayers. We need to oppose the New Age power of deception with the power of prayer. The kingdom of light is warring with the kingdom of darkness, Jesus Christ with Satan. And in this battle Jesus is counting on his faithful followers. They loyally fight at His side, and with their prayers they move the arm of God to draw many more souls out of the web of deception.[9]

Christians, then, are called to learn about the New Age, to listen and understand what its devotees are saying. Love them and share love and truth with them – pertinently and prayerfully. We are also concerned to live in the same world as New Agers. We cannot and we must not pretend such a movement doesn't exist. Nor must we allow ourselves to opt out of this world, for it belongs to God.

5. *Christians are concerned with the world now and in the future*

Jesus made it abundantly clear in the Sermon on the Mount that Christians are to be salt and light in today's world. We are to be light in the midst of darkness, and salt in those areas which would become rotten and decay. The New Age, as we have seen, has infiltrated into many areas of our national life – politics, science, health, psychology, advertising, the media, fashion, literature etc. Christians need to be positive and effective voices in all these areas of life today.

We need, also as Christians, to express joyfully and confidently our hope about the future of the world, and to look forward to the second coming of the Lord Jesus. The

Christian hope of our Lord's return is clearly and frequently predicted in the New Testament. (Such chapters as Matthew 25, Mark 13, Acts 1, the Epistles of Peter, and Paul's letters to the Thessalonians, as well as the whole message of the book of Revelation herald the truth that we are to affirm about the future of the world.)

It is quite clear, as Kate Saunders stated in her article in the *Sunday Times*, that conventional Christianity has no place in the New Age. The doctrine that God is a separate force from mankind is definitely old hat. New Agers feel we are all potentially godlike. Shirley MacLaine has whittled this down to 'I am God'.[10]

That is the crux of the conflict between New Age and Christianity. For it is the risen and ascended Jesus who in Revelation 1 states: 'I am the Alpha and the Omega, who is, and who was and who is to come, the Almighty . . . I am the first and the Last'; I am the Living one; I was dead, and behold I am alive for ever and ever! And I hold the keys of death and Hades' (Revelation 1:8, 17–18, NIV).

Because Christians are concerned with the Sovereignty of God – as well as with the truth, the right use of the mind, freedom and wholeness, evangelism and the current and future state of the world – we can be quietly confident that the true God is with us. We are certain of the victory that Jesus has won over Satan, and all his works and we can look forward to the decline of the so-called New Age movement with its claims of love, peace and personal fulfilment. We can experience, through Jesus alone, the New Life now, and ultimately the New Age that Jesus will usher in when, as the true Messiah and Christ, he comes again.

Notes

Chapter 1 Defining the New Age

1. John Allan, *Peace and Harmony* (Cubit, UCCF, Leicester, Spring 1988).
2. J. Gordon Melton, *The Encyclopedic Handbook of Cults in America* (Garland, New York and London, 1986), p. 110.
3. Allan, *op. cit.*
4. J. Gordon Melton, *op. cit.*
5. Douglas Groothuis, quoted in *Equipping the Saints* (Vineyard Ministries, Anaheim, Ca, Autumn 1988) from *Confronting the New Age Counterfeit* (Inter Varsity Press 1986).
6. J. Gordon Melton, *op. cit.*, p. 115.
7. Marilyn Ferguson, *The Aquarian Conspiracy* (Paladin Grafton Books, London, 1988).
8. Constance Cumbey, *The Hidden Dangers of the Rainbow* (Huntington House, Shreveport, Louisiana, 1983).
9. Fritjof Capra, *The Turning Point* (Collins Fontana, London, 1983).
10. David Spangler, *The Rebirth of the Sacred* (Gateway Books, Bath, 1984).
11. M. Basilea Schlink, *New Age* (The Evangelical Sisterhood of Mary, Darmstadt, 1988), p. 15.

Chapter 2 The Origins of the New Age

1. Letter from D. Garne, *Southend Standard Recorder* (20th October 1989).
2. Marilyn Ferguson, *The Aquarian Conspiracy* (Paladin Grafton Books, London, 1988), pp. 399f.
3. Quoted in C. E. Vulliamy, *John Wesley* (Epworth, London, 1954), p. 95.

4. Roy Carr and Tony Tyler, *The Beatles – An Illustrated Record* (London, 1978).

5. Quoted in Bob Larson, *Rock* (Tyndale House, Wheaton, Illinois, 1980).

6. Carr and Tyler, *op. cit.*

7. Ferguson, *op. cit.*, p. 250.

8. Laurel Robertson, quoted in Ferguson, *op. cit.*, p. 225.

9. Ferguson, *op. cit.*, p. 185.

10. *Ibid.*, p. 185.

11. *Ibid.*, p. 198.

12. *Ibid.*, pp. 197f.

13. *Ibid.*, p. 170.

14. *Ibid.*, pp. 410f.

15. *Ibid.*, p. 265.

16. *Ibid.*, p. 282.

17. *Ibid.*, p. 303.

18. *Ibid.*, pp. 93f.

19. *Ibid.*, pp. 412f.

20. Dom Robert Petitpierre (ed.), *Exorcism – The Findings of a Commission Convened by the Bishop of Exeter* (SPCK, London, 1972) quoted in John Richards, *But Deliver Us from Evil* (Darton, Longman and Todd, London, 1978), p. 19.

21. Frank Smyth, *Modern Witchcraft* (MacDonald Unit 75, 1970) quoted in Richards, *op. cit.*, pp. 20f.

22. Richards, *op. cit.*, pp. 28f.

23. *Ibid.*, pp. 29f.

24. Ferguson, *op. cit.*, p. 423.

25. *Ibid.*, p. 175.

26. Quoted in an article by John Vidal in *The Guardian* (19th August 1987).

27. Article by Mick Brown, 'A New Species Evolves', *Sunday Times* (25th August 1987).

Chapter 3 Man Becomes God

1. St Augustine (Confessions) quoted in *The History of Christianity* (Lion Publishing, Oxford, 1977), p. 198.

2. *Options*, November 1989. Feature entitled 'New Age London'.

3. Douglas Groothuis, *Unmasking the New Age* (Inter Varsity Press, Downers Grove, Illinois, 1986), p. 15.

    4. *Ibid.*, p. 13.
    5. C. S. Lewis, *Miracles*, pp. 82–83, quoted in *ibid.*, p. 49.
    6. Kevin Perrotta and Leanne Payne have written two articles in *Pastoral Renewal* (April and May 1988) and Leanne Payne's book, *The Healing Presence* (Crossway Books, Westchester, Illinois, 1989), develops the teaching.
    7. C. G. Jung, *Memories, Dreams and Reflections* (Random House, New York, 1973).
    8. Karen Hoyt (ed.), *The New Age Rage* (Fleming H. Revell, Old Tappan, New Jersey, 1987), p. 39.
    9. J. Gordon Melton, *The Encyclopedic Handbook of Cults in America* (Garland, New York and London, 1986), p. 112.
   10. Hoyt, *op. cit.*, p. 47.

Chapter 4 New Age as Religion

    1. M. Ferguson, *The Aquarian Conspiracy* (Paladin Grafton Books, London, 1988), p. 74.
    2. *Ibid.*, p. 84.
    3. Quoted in *ibid.*, p. 104.
    4. Abraham Maslow quoted in *ibid.*, p. 96.
    5. *Ibid.*, p. 17.
    6. *Ibid.*, p. 30.
    7. *Ibid.*, pp. 106f.
    8. *Ibid.*, p. 107.
    9. *Ibid.*, p. 107.
   10. Carl Jung quoted in *ibid.*, p. 116.
   11. *Ibid.*, p. 116.
   12. Frederick Flach quoted in *ibid.*, p. 117.
   13. *Ibid.*, pp. 420f.
   14. T. Higton, *Our God Reigns* (Hodder & Stoughton, London, 1988), pp. 16, 123–124, 130–132, 136, 237, 253.
   15. Ferguson, *op. cit.*, p. 406.
   16. *Alternatives: Winter/Spring Programme 1989* (St James's Church, Piccadilly), p. 1.
   17. *Ibid.*, p. 1.
   18. *Ibid.*, p. 2.
   19. *Ibid.*, p. 3.
   20. *Ibid.*, p. 2.
   21. F. L. Cross (ed.), *The Oxford Dictionary of the Christian Church* (Oxford University Press, London, 1963), pp. 1345–6.

22. *Alternatives: Winter/Spring Programme 1989*, p. 2.
23. *Ibid.*, p. 4.
24. Higton, *op. cit.*, pp. 112–137.
25. Romans 3:23 (GNB).
26. 1 John 4:8 (NIV).
27. 2 Timothy 4:8 (NIV).
28. Hebrews 4:12–13 (NIV).
29. 1 John 1:5–6 (NIV).
30. 1 Timothy 6:16 (NIV).
31. See for example John 1:1; 10:30–33; 20:28–29; Colossians 2:9 – which teaches Jesus's divinity; and Luke 2:40; 4:2, 6; 8:23; 24:42–43; John 11:35; 19:34 – which shows aspects of his humanity.
32. Matthew 27:46 (GNB).
33. 1 Peter 2:24 (NIV).
34. John 14:6 (NIV).
35. Galatians 5:2–4 (GNB).
36. *Serving Humanity* – a compilation from the works of Alice A. Bailey and The Tibetan Master, Djwhal Khul (Lucis Press Ltd, London, 1987), pp. 25, 421, 502, 411, 77.
37. *Ibid.*, p. 489.
38. *Ibid.*, p. 379.
39. *Ibid.*, p. 32.
40. *Ibid.*, p. 384.
41. *Ibid.*, p. 328.
42. *Ibid.*, p. 327.
43. *Ibid.*, p. 330.
44. *Ibid.*, p. 33.
45. *Ibid.*, p. 136.
46. *Ibid.*, pp. 33, 333.
47. *Ibid.*, p. 477.
48. *Ibid.*, pp. 338ff
49. *Ibid.*, p. 399.
50. *Ibid.*, p. 378.
51. *Ibid.*, p. 75.
52. 1 John 2:22.
53. 2 Thessalonians 2:3–11.
54. Higton, *op. cit.*, pp. 134ff.

Chapter 5 Reincarnation

1. *San Francisco Examiner*, 8 December 1977.
2. Bob Larson, *Larson's Book of Cults* (Tyndale House, Wheaton, Illinois, 1982), p. 51.
3. *Ibid.*, p. 77.
4. Autobiography of Lord Longford, *The Grain of Wheat*, 1974.
5. Charles Wesley, *1707–1788 Baptist Church Hymnal*, p. 174.
6. 'Dr Harry Rimmer's Farewell', Article in *Moody Monthly Magazine*.

Chapter 6 The Environment as Religion

1. *Songs of Praise*, BBC 1, 31st December 1989.
2. Quoted in *The Times*, 29th December 1989.
3. *Green Party UK Euro-Elections Broadsheet* (1989), p. 1.
4. *Don't let your World Turn Grey – The Green Party European Election Manifesto* (London, 1989), p. 26.
5. Quoted in Robert Whelan, *Mounting Greenery* (Institute of Economic Affairs, London, 1989), p. 18.
6. *Ibid.*, p. 18.
7. *Ibid.*, pp. 20ff.
8. *Ibid.*, p. 22.
9. *Ibid.*, p. 22.
10. Robert Theobald, *The Challenge of a Decade – Global Development or Global Breakdown* (UN, New York, 1969).
11. *Ibid.*, p. 9.
12. *Ibid.*, p. 11.
13. Hebrews 1:2–3.
14. Genesis 1:26–28.
15. Genesis 2:15 (NIV).
16. Exodus 23:10–12; Leviticus 25:1–7.
17. Leviticus 25:23–28.
18. Genesis 9:8–17 (NIV).
19. Genesis 3:17–19 (NIV).
20. J. Porritt, *The Coming of the Greens* (Fontana, London, 1988), p. 241.
21. Romans 8:18–25.
22. 2 Peter 3:10–12.
23. Romans 8:19–21.

24. 2 Peter 3:13; Revelation 21:1.
25. Porritt, *op. cit.*, p. 233.
26. J. Porritt, 'Let the Green Spirit Live!' article in *Link-up* magazine (Blockey, Glos., Spring 1989), p. 18.
27. Porritt, *The Coming of the Greens*, p. 240.
28. *Ibid.*, p. 242.
29. *Ibid.*, p. 246.
30. *Ibid.*, p. 238.
31. F. Capra, *Earth Island Journal* (1987), quoted in Porritt, *The Coming of the Greens*, pp. 238f.
32. Porritt, *The Coming of the Greens*, p. 247.
33. John Stewart Collis, *The Vision of Glory* (Penguin, London, 1975), quoted in Porritt, *The Coming of the Greens*, p. 251.
34. Richard North, *The Independent*, quoted in Porritt, *The Coming of the Greens*, pp. 251f.
35. Porritt, *The Coming of the Greens*, p. 253.
36. Peter Russell, 'Endangered Earth', article in *Link-up* magazine (Spring, 1989), p. 5.
37. *Ibid.*, p. 5.
38. Quoted in article by John Vidal, *The Guardian* (19th August 1987).
39. Advertisement for Wrekin Trust Conference in *Resurgence* magazine (Camelford, Cornwall, March/April, 1989), p. 59.
40. *Ibid.*, p. 59.
41. *Ibid.*, p. 59.
42. *Ibid.*, p. 59.
43. See Deuteronomy 18:10–12; Leviticus 19:31; 20:6.
44. Paul Hawken, *The Magic of Findhorn* (Fontana/Souvenir Press, London, 1988), pp. 48ff.
45. *Ibid.*, pp. 186f, 191, 197.
46. *Ibid.*, p. 146.
47. *Ibid.*, p. 118.
48. *Ibid.*, p. 127.
49. *Ibid.*, p. 141.
50. *Ibid.*, p. 144.
51. *Ibid.*, p. 156.
52. *Ibid.*, p. 150.
53. *Ibid.*, pp. 171ff.
54. *Ibid.*, p. 193.
55. *Ibid.*, p. 195.
56. *Ibid.*, p. 198.

Chapter 7 The World Conspiracy Theory

1. Marilyn Ferguson, *The Aquarian Conspiracy* (Paladin Grafton Books, London, 1988), pp. 62–63.
2. *Options*, November 1989, p. 3.
3. M. Basilea Schlink, *New Age* (The Evangelical Sisterhood of Mary, Darmstadt, 1988), p. 11.
4. Constance E. Cumbey, *The Hidden Dangers of the Rainbow* (Huntington House, Shreveport, Louisiana, 1983), pp. 20, 56 and 124.
5. Douglas Groothuis, *Unmasking the New Age* (Inter Varsity Press, Downers Grove, Illinois, 1986), p. 127.
6. *Ibid.*, pp. 47–48.
7. Karen Hoyt (ed.), *The New Age Rage* (Fleming H. Revell, Old Tappan, New Jersey, 1987), pp. 186–187.
8. *Ibid.*, p. 193.
9. *Ibid.*, p. 194.
10. Basilea Schlink, *op. cit.*, p. 18.
11. Groothuis, *op. cit.*, p. 111.
12. *Ibid.*, p. 122.

Chapter 8 'Spiritual Powers' – Genuine and Counterfeit

1. This paragraph summarises my much more detailed discussion of such physical phenomena in: David C. Lewis, *Healing: Fiction, Fantasy or Fact?* (Hodder & Stoughton, London, 1989), chapter 4.
2. See also Douglas McBain, *Eyes that See: The Spiritual Gift of Discernment* (Marshall Pickering, Basingstoke, 1986).
3. Quoted from Lewis, *op. cit.*, p. 339, footnote 47.
4. This is the Bradburn scale: see Norman M. Bradburn, *The Structure of Psychological Wellbeing* (Aldine Press, Chicago, 1969).
5. The relevant spiritual experiences were described in terms such as being 'bathed in light' or having 'new life', involving also an inability to express the experiences adequately in human language and a sense that the 'active' agent in the experience was the encountered 'Other'. See Andrew M. Greeley and William C. McCready, *The Mystical, the Twice Born and the Happy: An Investigation of the Sociology of Religious Experience* (National Opinion Research Center, University of Chicago, 1974) and David Hay, *Exploring Inner Space* (A. R. Mowbray, Oxford and London, 1987), pp. 173–174.

6. Some examples of these 'other' experiences have been published in my article: David C. Lewis, 'All in Good Faith', *Nursing Times* and *Nursing Mirror* (London, 18th–24th March 1987), pp. 40–43.

7. $p = <0.05$, by a statistical method known as the analysis of variance. The chances of such a result occurring by chance are less than five out of a hundred.

8. None of the nurses belonged to the Jehovah's Witnesses.

9. This takes into account the fact that some people are not allowed to give blood on medical grounds.

10. *The Independent*, Saturday 17th March 1990, p. 4; *Prophecy Today* (vol. 3, no. 5, September/October 1987), p. 17.

11. John Wimber with Kevin Springer, *Power Healing* (Hodder & Stoughton, London, 1986), pp. 111–112, 122–127.

12. Bill Musk, *The Unseen Face of Islam* (Monarch Publications, Eastbourne, 1989), p. 115.

13. *Ibid.*, p. 240.

14. Hendrik G. Boerenkamp, 'A Study of Paranormal Impressions of Psychics', *European Journal of Parapsychology* (vol. 5, 1985), pp. 327–371.

15. Personal communication from Dr Alan Gauld, senior lecturer in psychology, University of Nottingham.

16. John Dale and Richard Holliday, 'Doubting Doris', *The Mail on Sunday*, (20th April 1986).

17. John Dale and Richard Holliday, 'Cheated Mother's Despair', *The Mail on Sunday* (27th April 1986). The details about Doris Stokes sending the complimentary tickets and train fare were supplied in a personal communication to me from John Dale, one of the journalists who reported this.

18. David C. Lewis, 'Religious Rites in a Japanese Factory', *Japanese Journal of Religious Studies* (vol. 13, no. 4, 1986).

19. Michael Shallis, 'Electricity and Health', *Caduceus* (Issue no. 3, 1988).

Chapter 9 Is Christian 'Renewal' Really 'New Age' in Disguise?

1. Dave Hunt and T. C. McMahon, *The Seduction of Christianity* (Harvest House Publishers, Eugene, Oregon, 1985).

2. David Pytches, *Does God Speak Today?* (Hodder & Stoughton, London, 1989).

3. Morton Kelsey, *The Christian and the Supernatural* (Search Press, London, 1977).

4. Peter Masters, 'The Texts all say No!', *Sword & Trowel*, (no. 1, 1987), pp. 18, 20–21, 28–29.

5. Pytches, *op. cit.*, pp. 44–46.

6. David C. Lewis, *Healing: Fiction, Fantasy or Fact?* (Hodder & Stoughton, London, 1989), pp. 132–133.

7. *Ibid.*, pp. 133–135.

8. S. G. Soal and F. Bateman, *Modern Experiments in Telepathy* (Faber & Faber, London, 1954), p. 313.

9. D. J. West, *Psychical Research Today* (Penguin Books, Harmondsworth, 1962), pp. 133, 147–148.

10. John Gunstone, *Signs & Wonders: The Wimber Phenomenon* (Daybreak imprint, Darton, Longman & Todd, London, 1989), p. 103.

11. Don Matzat, *Inner Healing: Deliverance or Deception?* (Harvest House Publishers, Eugene, Oregon, 1987).

12. Paul Yonggi Cho, *The Fourth Dimension* (Logos International, Plainfield, New Jersey, 1979), p. 42.

13. John Wimber with Kevin Springer, *Power Healing* (Hodder & Stoughton, London, 1986), p. 285.

14. Rita Bennett, *How to Pray for Inner Healing for Yourself and Others* (Kingsway Publications, Eastbourne, 1984), pp. 36–45.

15. D. Lewis, *Healing: Fiction, Fantasy or Fact?* chapter 2.

16. *Ibid.*, pp. 75–76, 187.

17. Rex Gardner, *Healing Miracles: A Doctor Investigates* (Darton, Longman & Todd, London, 1986), pp. 175–184; Francis MacNutt, *Healing* (Ave Maria Press, Notre Dame, Indiana, 1974), pp. 327–333.

18. David Pytches, *Come, Holy Spirit* (Hodder & Stoughton, London, 1985), p. 250.

19. For this insight into the ways in which 'inner healing' was also involved in the healing of the woman with menhorragia, I am grateful to Peter Horrobin, Director of Ellel Grange, a healing centre in Lancashire. He pointed this out in one of his talks at a conference entitled 'The Battle Belongs to the Lord' held in Brighton in February 1990.

20. Summarised from John Wimber's public accounts at his 'Spiritual Warfare' conference in Anaheim, February 1989, and his 'Worship' conference in Brighton, October 1989.

21. Summarised from Mike Bickle's references to Bob Jones at the 'Spiritual Warfare' conference mentioned above and from David Pytches, *Some Said It Thundered* (Hodder & Stoughton, London, 1990), pp. 89–90.

Chapter 10 Comparing Christianity and New Age

1. Paul McGuire, *Evangelizing the New Age* (Vine Books – Servant Publications, Ann Arbor), p. 11.

2. Dr William Barclay, *When we Pray* (Collins Fontana), p. 10

3. *Thistlewood, The Cato Street Conspirator* – quoted by G. R. Balleine in *What Jesus Said* (Home Words, London), p. 132.

4. Quoted by Murdo Ewen McDonald in *The Need to Believe* (Collins Fontana, London, 1959), p. 7.

5. *Ibid.*, p. 8.

6. *Ibid.*, p. 12.

7. Norman Grubb, *C. T. Studd: Cricketer and Pioneer* (Lutterworth Press, Cambridge, 1982).

8. *Ibid.*

9. *Westwood: Fleming H. Ravell* – quoted by Josh McDowell in *Evidence that Demands a Verdict* (Campus Crusade, San Bernardino, California, 1979), p. 133.

10. Quoted by Josh McDowell in *Evidence that Demands a Verdict*, *op. cit.*, p. 133.

11. Noel Richards, 'He Laid Aside His Majesty', Copyright Thank You Music 1985.

12. Sholem Ash, cited by Frank Mead in *The Encyclopedia of Religious Quotations*.

13. C. S. Lewis, quoted by Josh McDowell, *op. cit.*, p. 107.

14. William Shakespeare, *Measure for Measure*, Act V, scene 1.

15. Dostoevsky, *The Brothers Karamazov* – quoted by Murdo Ewen MacDonald in *The Need to Believe*, *op. cit.*, p. 53.

Chapter 11 The Real New Age

1. Goethe, quoted by William Barclay in *The Promise of the Spirit* (Westminster John Knox, Philadelphia, 1978), p. 106.

2. Quoted by Stephen Trains, *The Jesus Hope* (Word, 1974), p. 9.

3. Dr William Barclay, *New Testament Words* (S.C.M., London, 1964), p. 45.

4. J. S. Stewart, *The Strong Name* (Hodder & Stoughton, London, 1973), p. 243.

5. Robert Lowry, *1826–1899 Baptist Church Hymnal*, p. 202.

6. William Golding, *Lord of the Flies* – quoted by David C. K. Watson in *My God is Real* (Falcon Books, Eastbourne, 1978), p. 23.

7. J. I. Packer, *I Want to be a Christian* (Kingsway Pubns, Eastbourne, 1985), pp. 95–96.

8. Murdo Ewen MacDonald, *The Call to Obey* (Hodder & Stoughton, London, 1963), p. 50.

9. John 1, vs. 26–35.

10. A story I have recalled.

11. Quoted by Jim Graham, *The Giant Awakes* (Marshalls, London, 1982), p. 21.

12. John Owen, *Works of John Owen*, vol. 4 (Banner of Truth, Carlisle, Pennsylvania, 1980), p. 432.

13. Emil Brunner, *The Misunderstanding of the Church*, p. 50.

14. Dr John MacBeath, *The Life of a Christian* (Marshall, Morgan & Scott, London), p. 71.

15. G. T. Manley, *The Return of Jesus Christ* (IVF, London, 1960), p. 20.

16. Horatio G. Spafford, 1828–1888.

Chapter 12 Putting on the Armour

1. J. Melton Gordon, *The Encyclopedic Handbook of Cults in America* (Garland, New York and London, 1986), p. 107.

2. Karen Hoyt (ed.), *The New Age Rage* (Fleming H. Revell, Old Tappan, New Jersey, 1987), p. 227.

3. *Ibid.*, p. 12.

4. M. Basilea Schlink, *New Age* (The Evangelical Sisterhood of Mary, Darmstadt, 1988), p. 6.

5. Douglas Groothuis, *Unmasking the New Age* (Inter Varsity Press, Downers Grove, Illinois, 1986), p. 146.

6. Basilea Schlink, *op. cit.*, p. 8.

7. *Ibid.*, p. 8–10.

8. Evangelical Alliance, Action Agenda for Church Representatives, October 1989.

9. Basilea Schlink, *op. cit.*, p. 28.

10. Kate Saunders, 'All you need is self-love', *Sunday Times*, 29th October 1989.